Rugby
in the Office

Also available in Sphere Books:

RUGBY JOKES
SON OF RUGBY JOKES
MORE RUGBY JOKES
WHAT RUGBY JOKES DID NEXT
EVEN MORE RUGBY JOKES
RUGBY JOKES SCORE AGAIN
HANDS UP FOR RUGBY JOKES
RUGBY SONGS
MORE RUGBY SONGS

Rugby Jokes in the Office

*Illustrated by
Raymond Turvey*

SPHERE BOOKS LIMITED

A SPHERE BOOK

First published in Great Britain
by Sphere Books Ltd 1989

This selection and editorial matter
copyright © 1989 by E.L. Ranelagh
Cartoon copyright © 1989 by Raymond Turvey

All rights reserved.
No part of this publication may be reproduced,
stored in a retrieval system, or transmitted, in any
form or by any means without the prior
permission in writing of the publisher, nor be
otherwise circulated in any form of binding or
cover other than that in which it is published and
without a similar condition including this
condition being imposed on the subsequent
purchaser.

Reproduced, printed and bound in Great Britain by
Richard Clay Ltd, Bungay, Suffolk

Sphere Books Ltd
A Division of
Macdonald & Co (Publishers) Ltd.
66/73 Shoe Lane, London EC4P 4AB
A member of Maxwell Pergamon Publishing Corporation plc

Contents

CHAPTER 1
Up the Chain of Command 9

CHAPTER 2
Down the Chain of Command 27

CHAPTER 3
Job Relations 51

CHAPTER 4
For the Working Woman 73

CHAPTER 5
For the Working Man 93

CHAPTER 6
International Relations 103

CHAPTER 7
You're Never Too Old (And You're Never Too Young) 113

CHAPTER 8
Belts from the Bible 127

"Welcome Gentlemen, to Advanced Management Training"

CHAPTER 1

Up the Chain of Command

UP THE CHAIN OF COMMAND

Up the System:

DOWN THE CHAIN OF COMMAND

The Chain of Command

IF YOU WANT TO GET TO THE TOP

Get off your bottom

The Six Project Stages

- *Wild enthusiasm*
- *Disillusionment*
- *Total confusion*
- *Search for the guilty*
- *Punishment of the innocent*
- *Promotion of the non-participants*

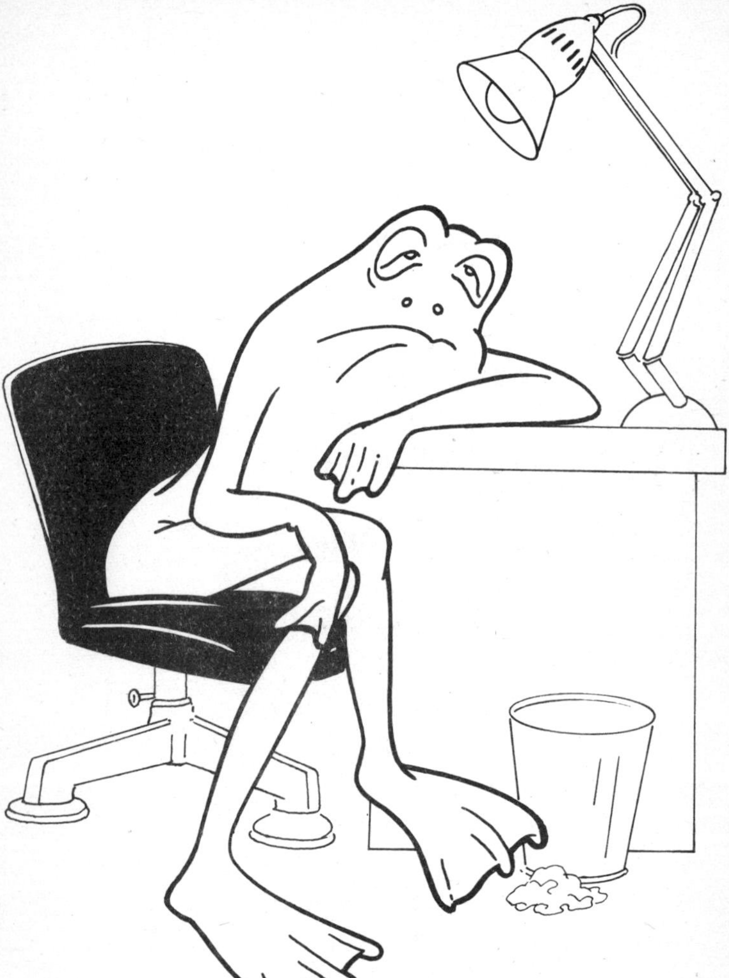

I'M SO
HAPPY HERE
I COULD
JUST SHIT

Mmmm — no wonder everybody chews on it,
IT'S DELICIOUS!!

This is a saluting base

ABOUT COMMUNICATIONS:

As Marketing Requested It

As Sales Ordered It!

As Engineering Designed It

As Manufactured

As Plant Installed It

What The Customer Ordered

It's hard to soar with EAGLES when you work with TURKEYS!

*"SHALL I RUSH this rush job before
I rush the rush job I'm rushing now?"*

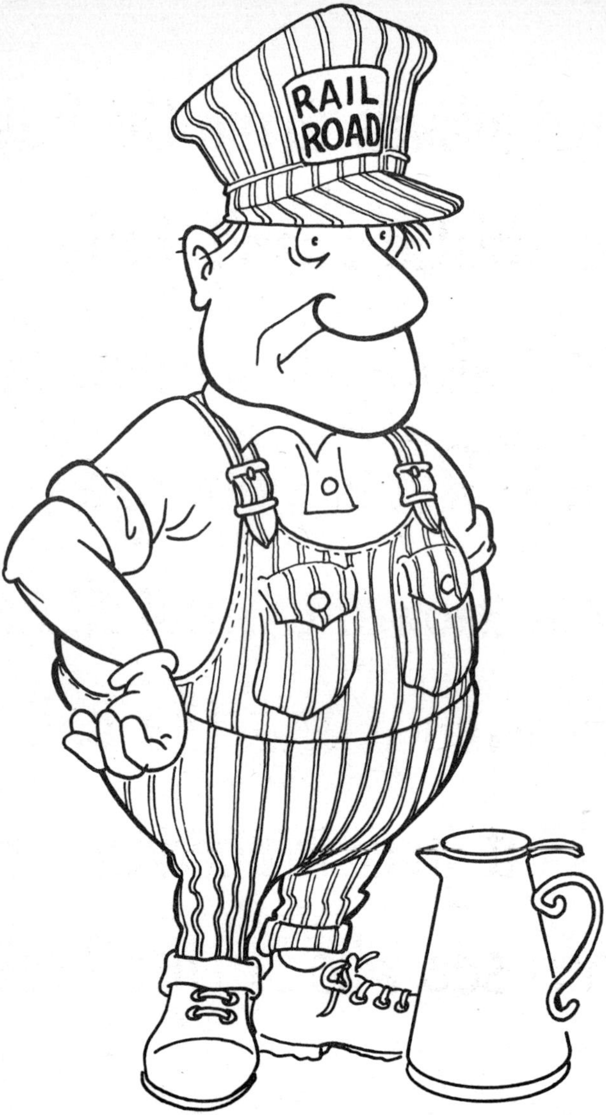
RAIL
ROAD

I'm not allowed to run the train
The whistle I can't blow
I'm not allowed to say how far
The R.R. cars can go
I'm not allowed to shoot off steam
Nor even clang the bell
But let it jump the goddam track
Then see who catches hell!

"I QUIT!!"

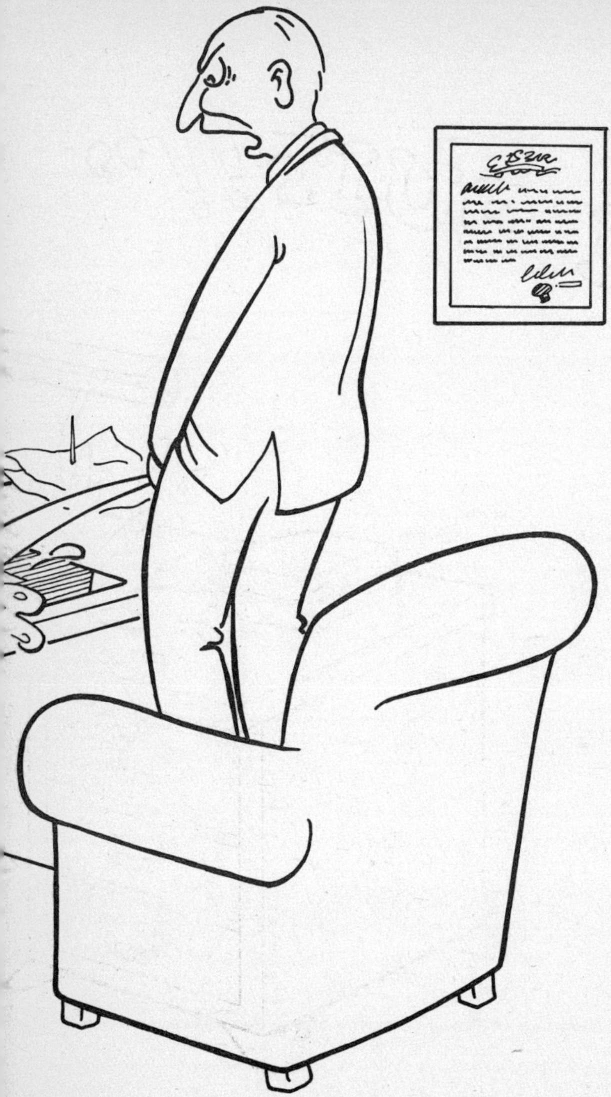

CHAPTER 2

Down the Chain of Command

*THE ONLY MAN AROUND HERE
WHO KNOWS WHAT HE IS DOING!*

PLEASE DON'T DROP CIGARETTE BUTTS ON THE FLOOR ...
The cockroaches are dying of CANCER

*The ratrace is over!
The rats won!*

Mike, I see you are having a good day!

Don't think of me
as inefficient!

My job is so secret,
it doesn't allow me to know
what I am doing

Take heart!

*The only person who
ever got all his work done
by Friday was*

ROBINSON CRUSOE

CERTIF

for your very
performance you

"One

One thousand "attaboys"
a leader of men, work
explain assorted problems
be looked upon as a local

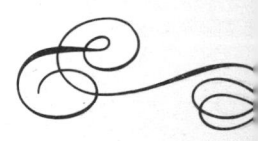

Note: One "awshit" wipes the
all over

ICATE

outstanding
are awarded

Attaboy"

qualifies you to be
overtime with a smile,
to management and
hero, without a raise in pay.

board clean and you must start
again.

ANSWERS PRICE LIST

ANSWERS   75p

ANSWERS
(requiring thought)   £1.25

ANSWERS
(correct)   £2.15

DUMB LOOKS ARE STILL FREE

The Last Great Act of Defiance

RUSH JOB CALENDAR

Neg	Fri	Fri	Fri	Thu	Wed	Tue
8	7	6	5	4	3	2
16	15	14	12	11	10	9
23	22	21	20	19	18	17
32	30	28	27	26	25	24
39	38	37	36	35	34	33

1. This is a special calendar for handling rush jobs. All rush jobs are wanted yesterday. With this calendar a job can be ordered on the 7th and delivered on the third.
2. Most jobs are required by Friday, so there are three Fridays in every week.
3. There are eight new days added to each month to allow for end-of-the-month panic jobs.
4. There is no first of the month — thus avoiding late delivery of the previous month's last minute panic jobs.
5. Monday morning hangovers are abolished together with non-productive Saturdays and Sundays.
6. A new day — Negotiation Day — has been introduced keeping the other days free for uninterrupted 'panic'.

*I think I'm a mushroom
because they keep me in the dark
and feed me bullshit!*

Cows may come,

and cows may go . . .

But the <u>BULL</u> in this place

goes on forever!

THIS JOB KEEPS CUTTING INTO MY DAY!

*Never try to teach a pig to sing;
it wastes your time and it annoys the pig.*

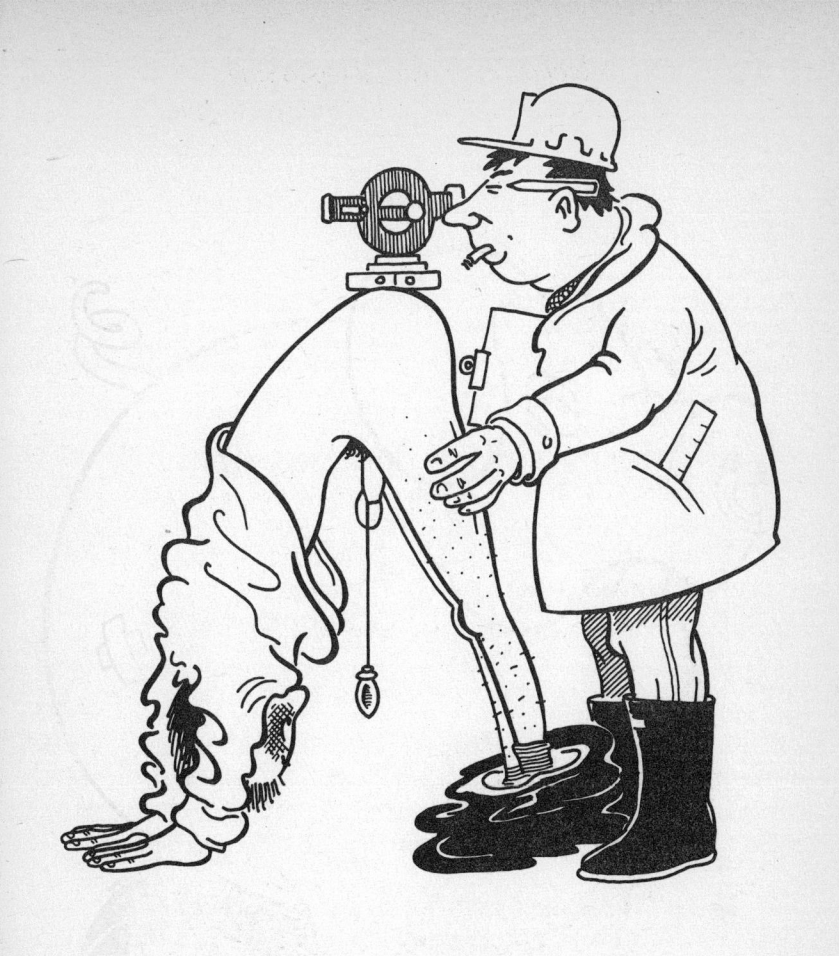

I'll bet the next time you won't forget that god-damned tripod, Tom.

TELEPHONE MESSAGE

TO _____

TIME _____ DATE _____

MR. _____

COMPANY _____

PHONE NO. _____ EXT. _____

While You Were Fucking Around
OR

☐ Drinking Coffee   ☐ Helling Around
☐ At the Beer Joint   ☐ Playing Golf
☐ Asleep   ☐ Masturbating

YOUR

☐ Bookie   ☐ Boss   ☐ Girl's father
☐ Wife   ☐ Mother-in-law   ☐ Broker
☐ Brunette   ☐ Blonde   ☐ Pal
☐ Secretary   ☐ Banker   ☐ Red Head

CALLED AND LEFT WORD FOR YOU TO —

☐ Get to work   ☐ Bring out the quart
☐ Come by her apartment   ☐ Marry the girl
☐ Her husband came home   ☐ Get the hell out of town

☐ Send cheque   ☐ Pay ....
☐ Bring home some .... ☐ Renew that note

*When the going gets tough,
the tough go to lunch.*

DUE TO THE
OUTBREAK OF
AIDS,
EMPLOYEES
WILL NO
LONGER BE
PERMITTED TO
KISS THE
BOSS'S ASS!

"I don't know what you guys see in these computers..."

We are running
your idea
through proper channels.

ONE FLUSH SHOULD DO IT!

"Boy, was I drunk last night! I don't even remember your name!"

CHAPTER 3

Job Relations

NEVER
PISS OFF A DICKEY BIRD!

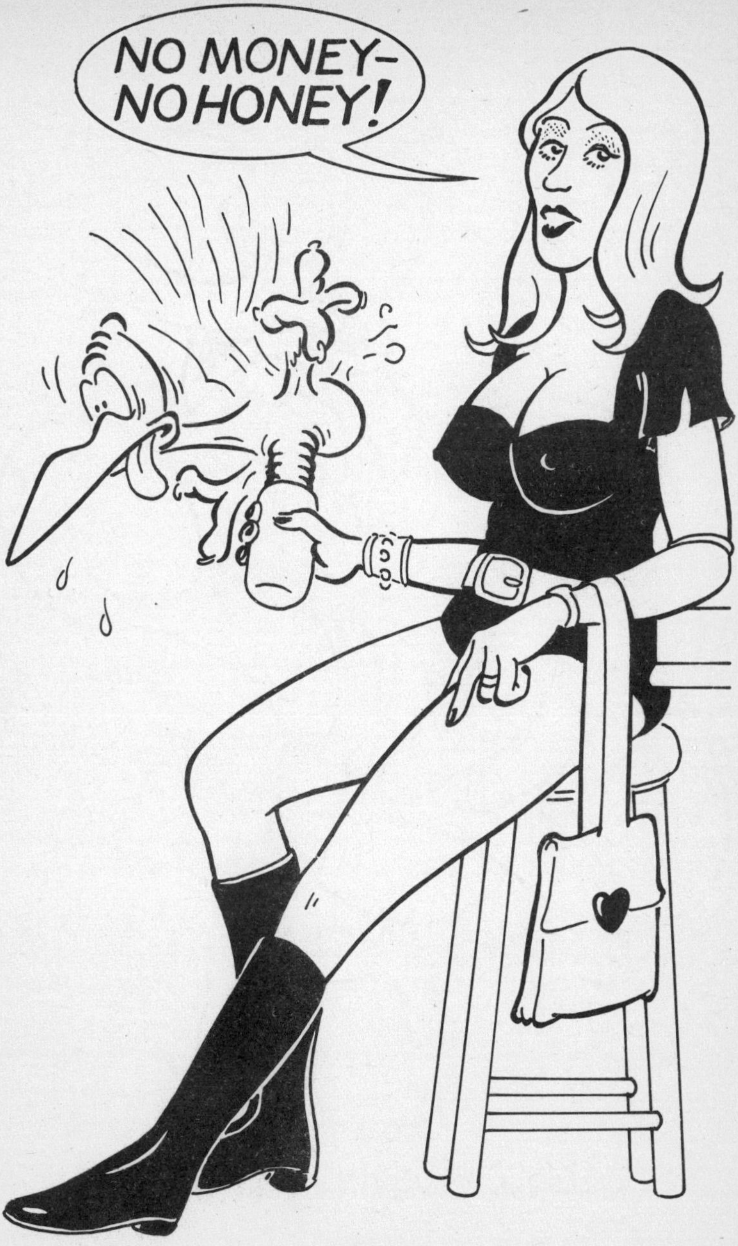
NO MONEY-
NO HONEY!

The Dickey Bird and his prey ...

THE DICKEY BIRD STRIKES AGAIN!

Coo! Flamin' iron knickers!

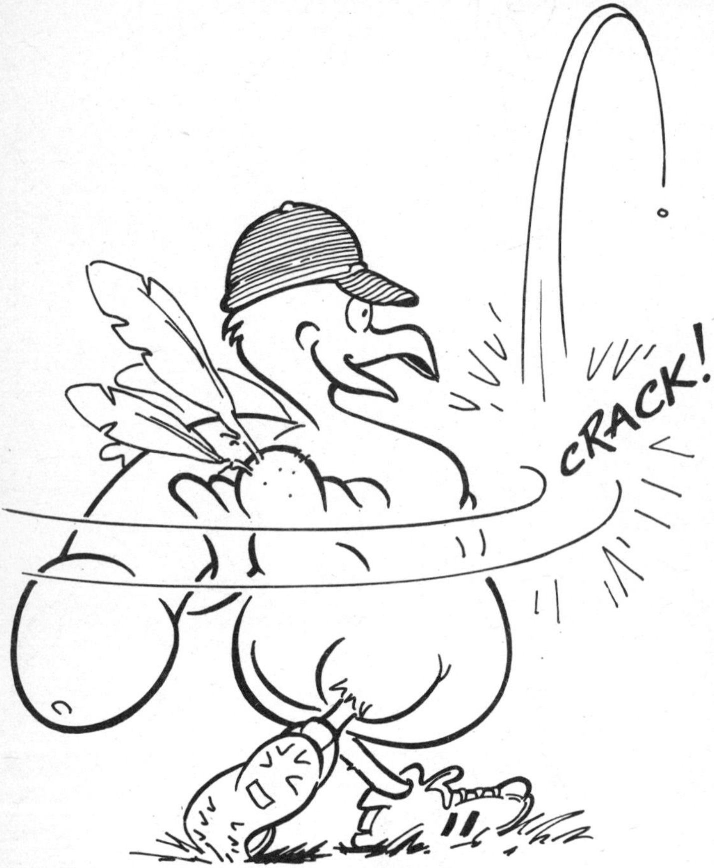
CRACK!

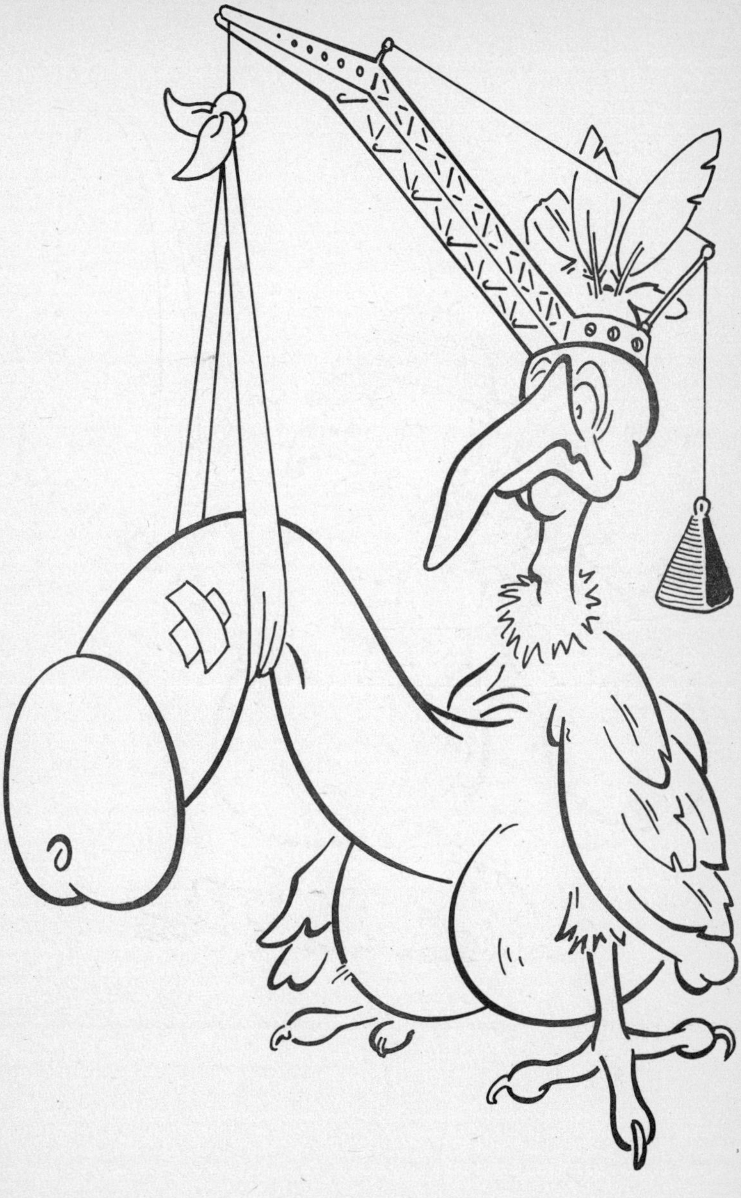

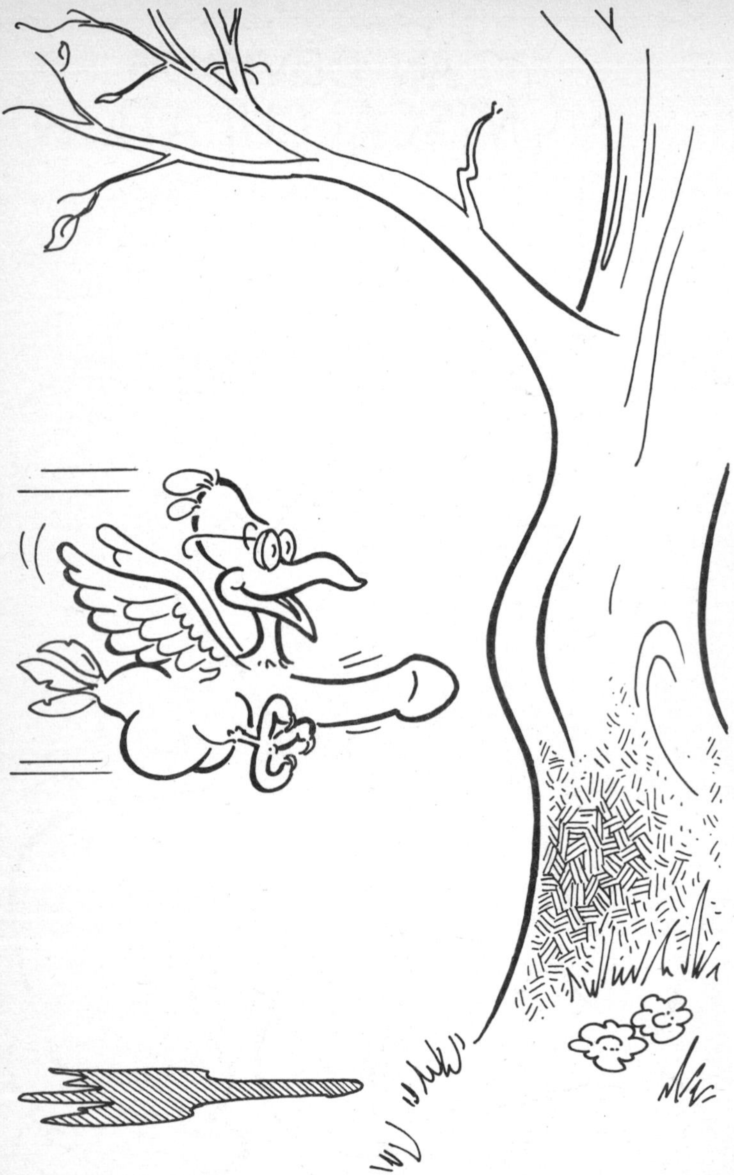

AN OBVIOUS MISCALCULATION

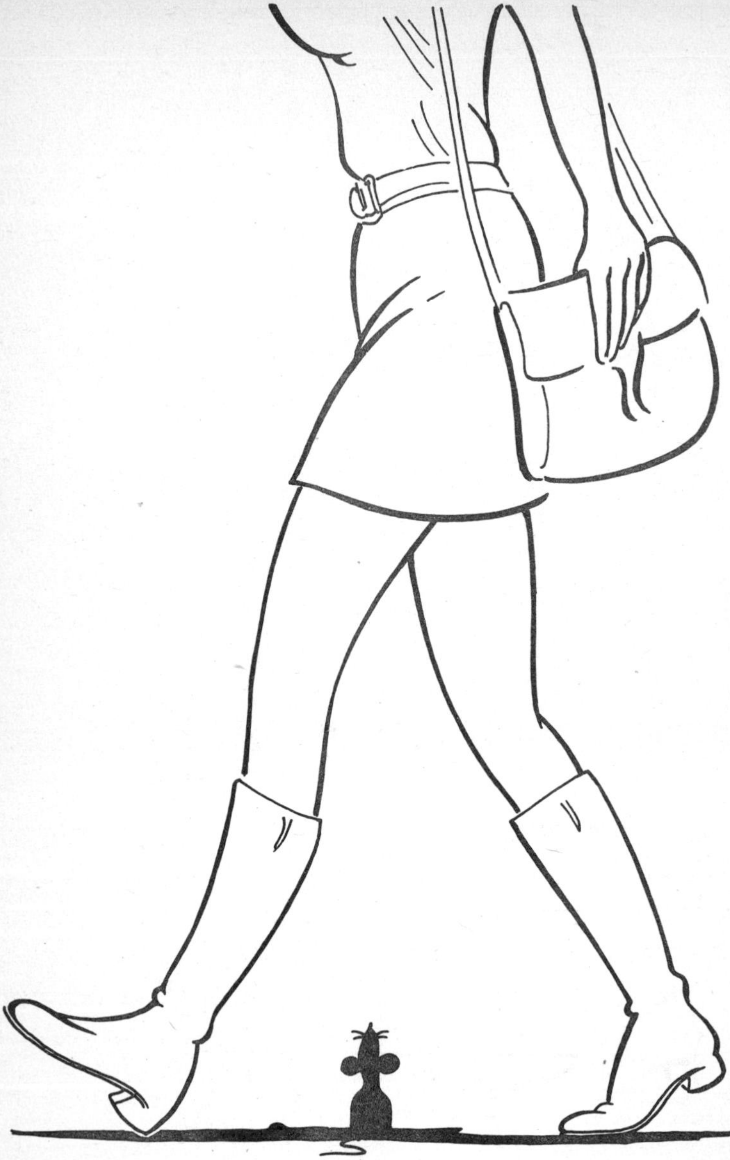

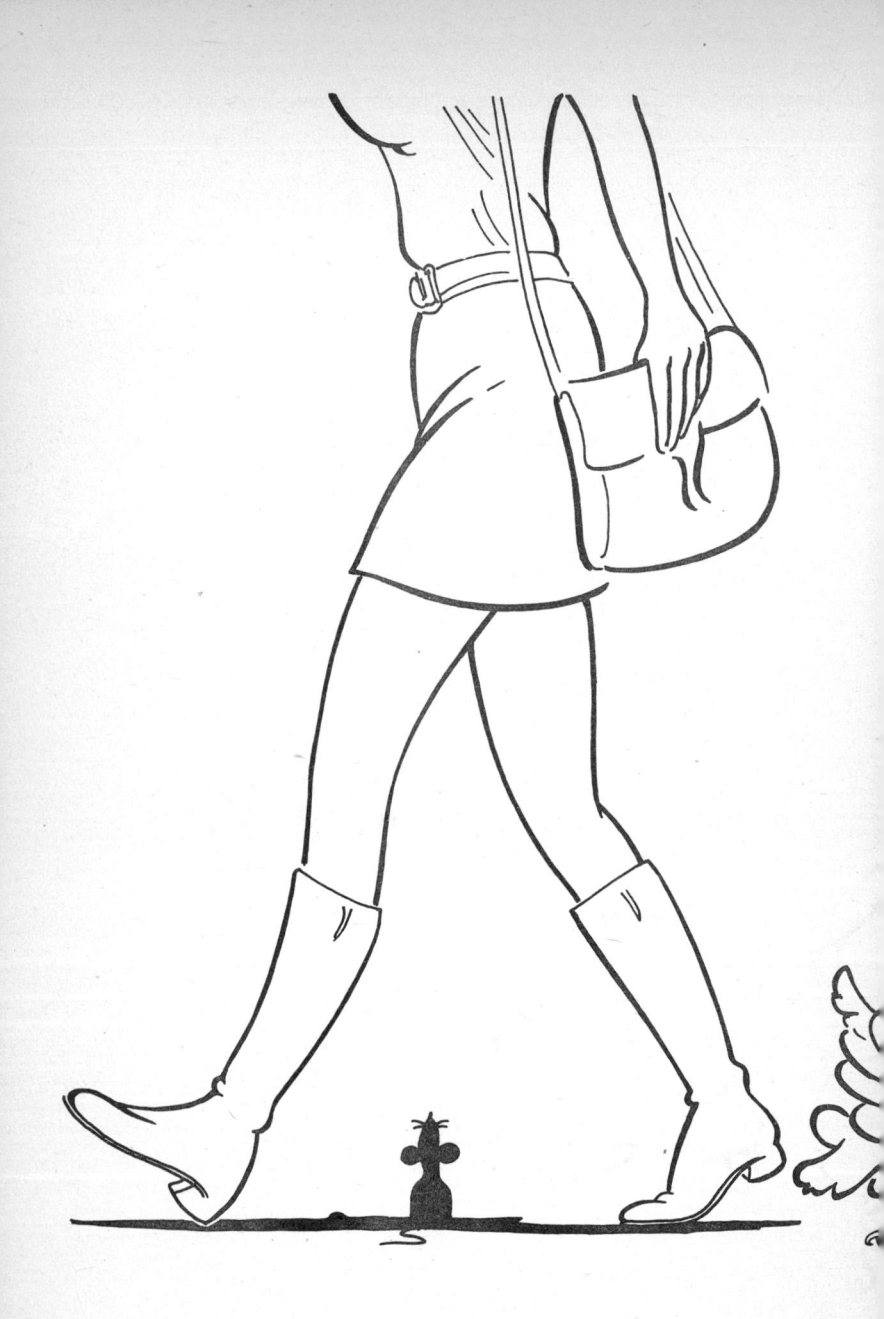

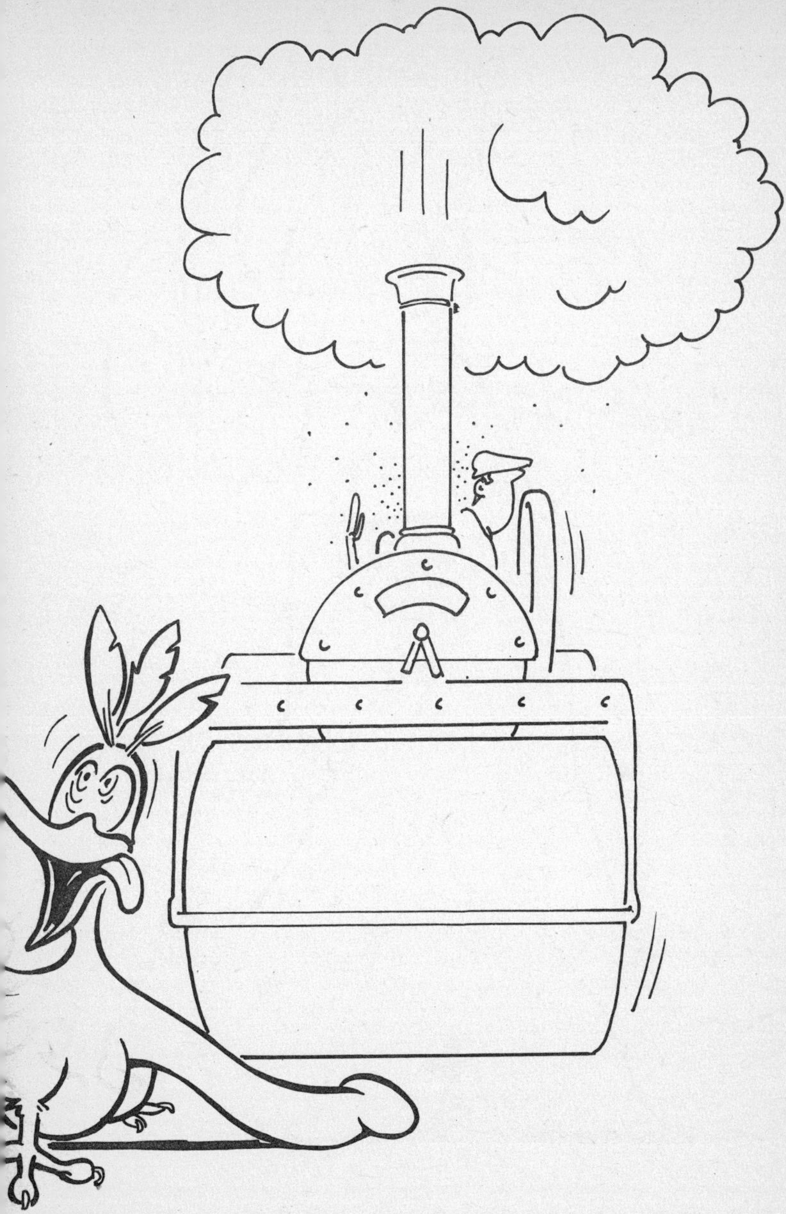

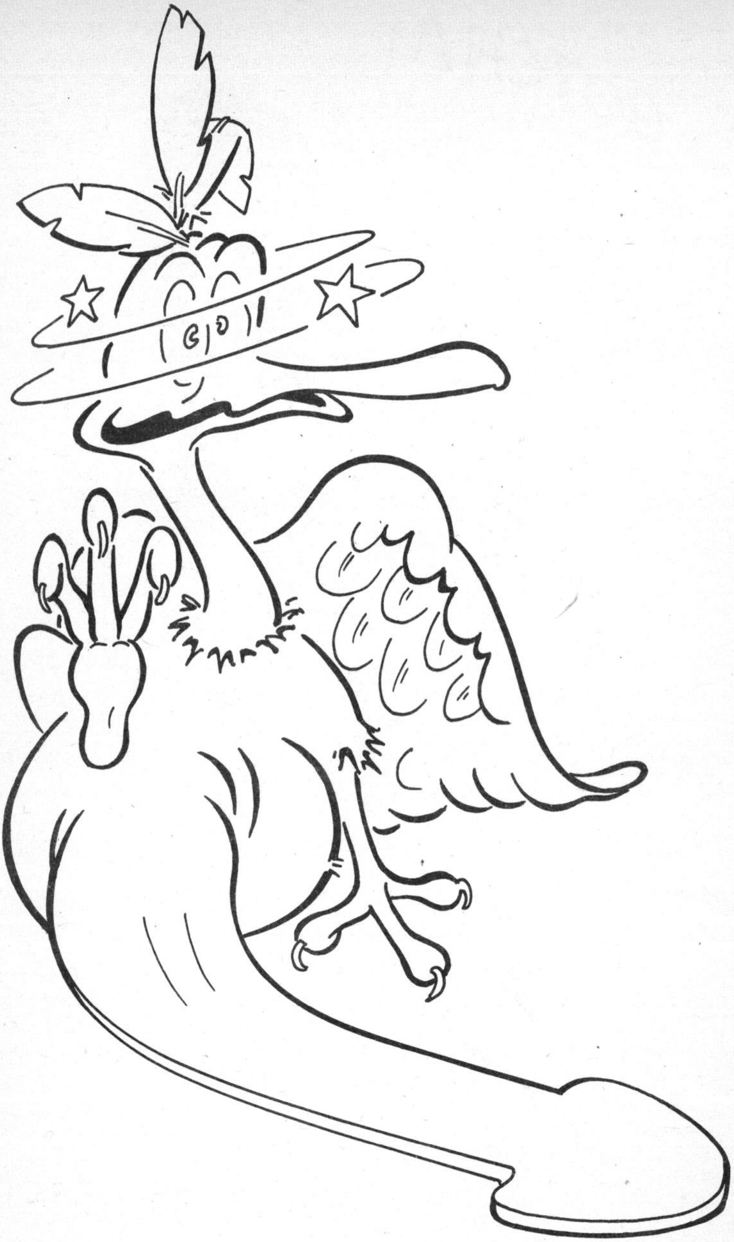

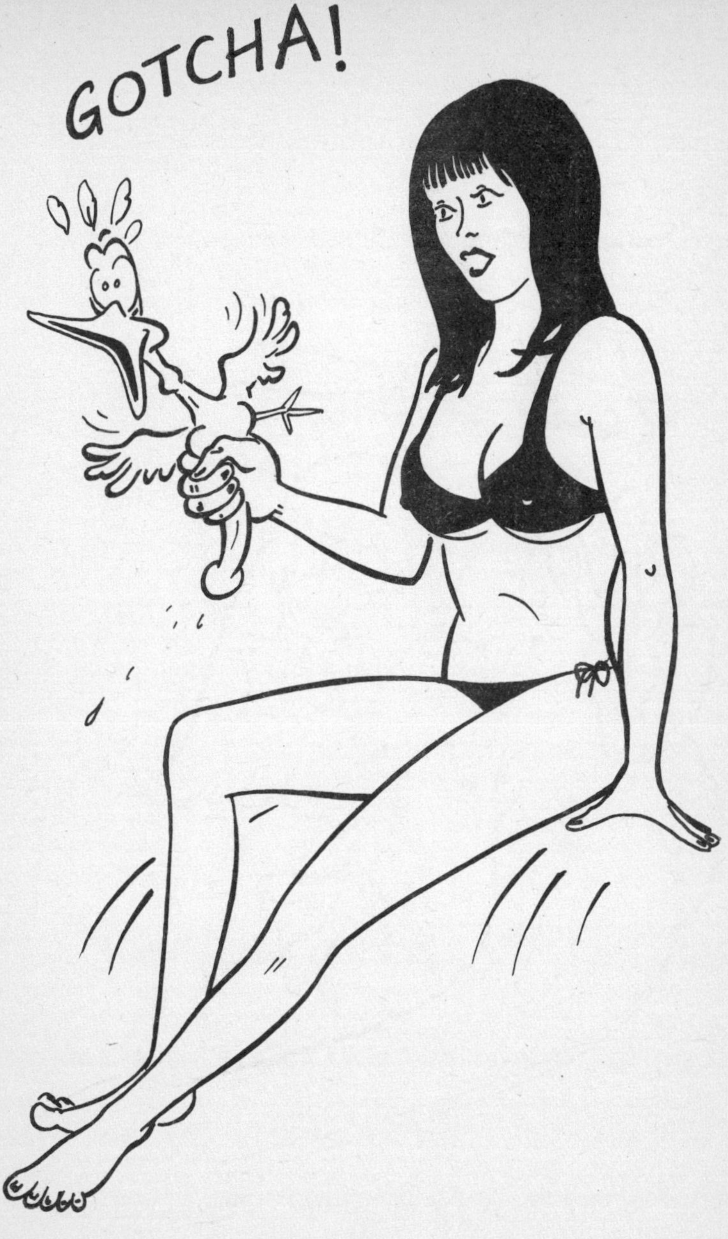
GOTCHA!

SHIT! and to think I'm only $12\frac{1}{2}$ *years old.*

*Everyone should believe
in something;*

I believe I'll have another beer.

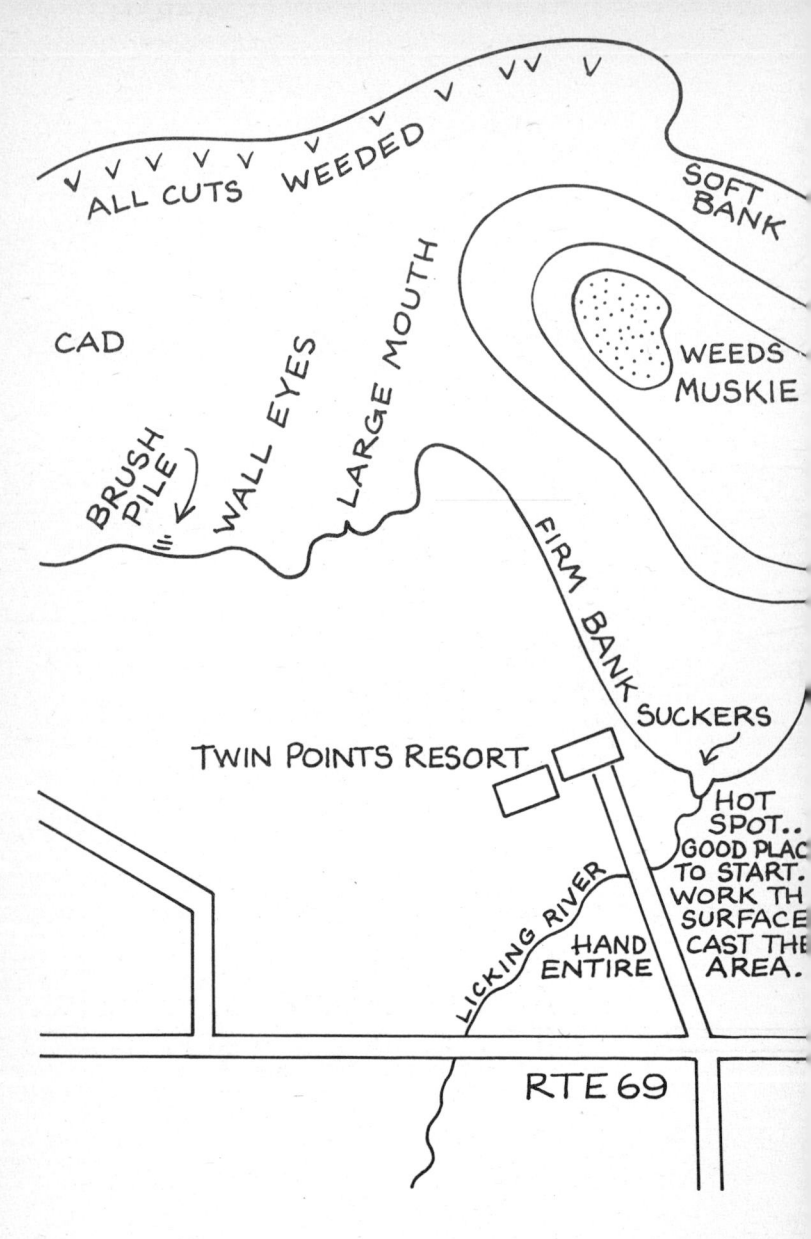
ALL CUTS WEEDED
SOFT BANK
CAD
WALL EYES
LARGE MOUTH
WEEDS
MUSKIE
BRUSH PILE
FIRM BANK
SUCKERS
TWIN POINTS RESORT
HOT SPOT..
GOOD PLAC
TO START.
WORK TH
SURFACE
CAST THE
AREA.
LICKING RIVER
HAND
ENTIRE
RTE 69

MARSH

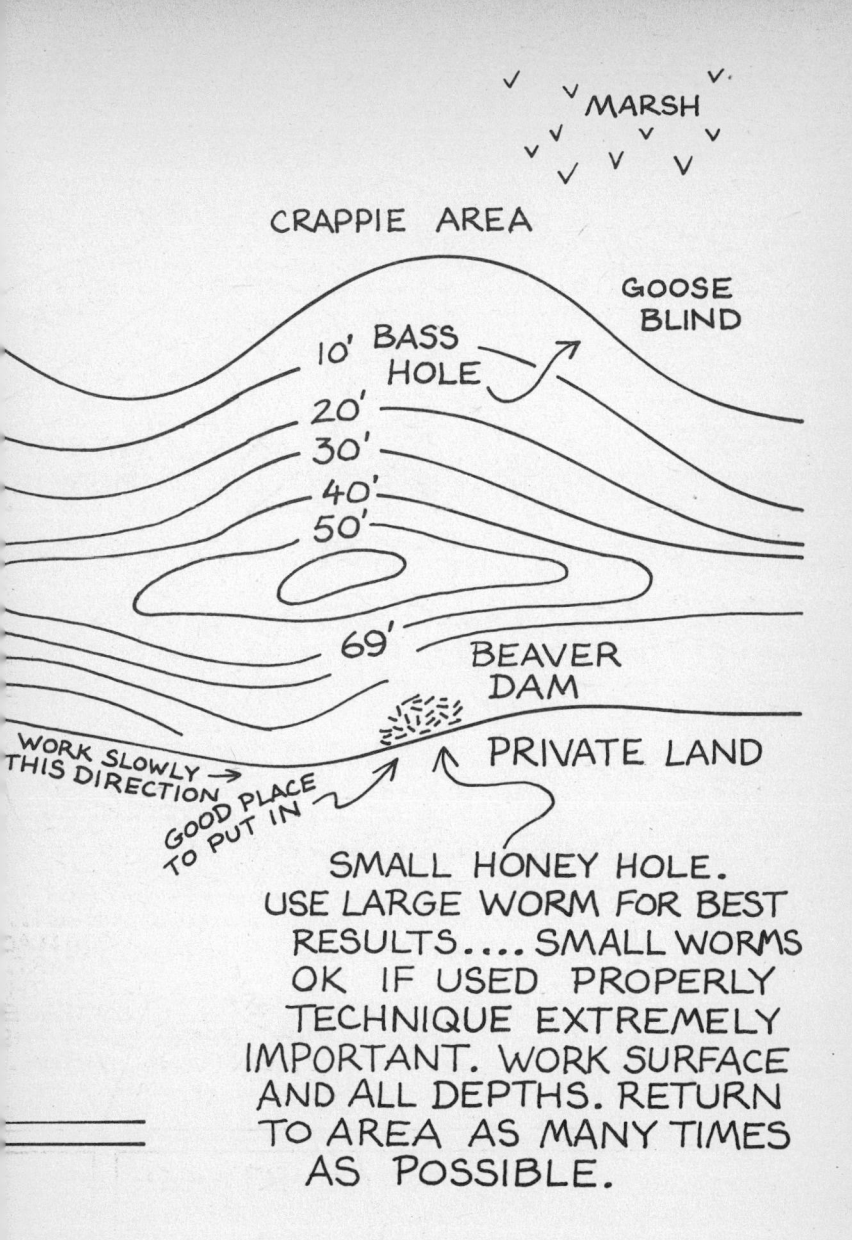

CRAPPIE AREA

10' BASS HOLE
GOOSE BLIND
20'
30'
40'
50'
69'
BEAVER DAM

WORK SLOWLY THIS DIRECTION →
GOOD PLACE TO PUT IN
PRIVATE LAND

SMALL HONEY HOLE. USE LARGE WORM FOR BEST RESULTS.... SMALL WORMS OK IF USED PROPERLY TECHNIQUE EXTREMELY IMPORTANT. WORK SURFACE AND ALL DEPTHS. RETURN TO AREA AS MANY TIMES AS POSSIBLE.

PERMANENT WRINKLES
FROM CONSTANT SMILE
AND DEADLINE PRESSURE

HARD OF HEARING FROM
EXPOSURE TO TELEPHONE
DUTY AND DICTAPHONE

LOSS OF TEETH DUE
TO LACK OF TIME FOR
DENTAL APPOINTMENTS

FINGER CANCER
FROM TOO MANY
REWRITES, RETYPES
AND PAPER CUTS

ULCER FROM HOLDING
BACK URGE TO PUNCH
SOMEBODY OUT

TACKY CLOTHES
FROM 25 YEARS
OF LOW PAY

TENNIS SHOES TO RUN
AFTER (OR FROM) BOSS

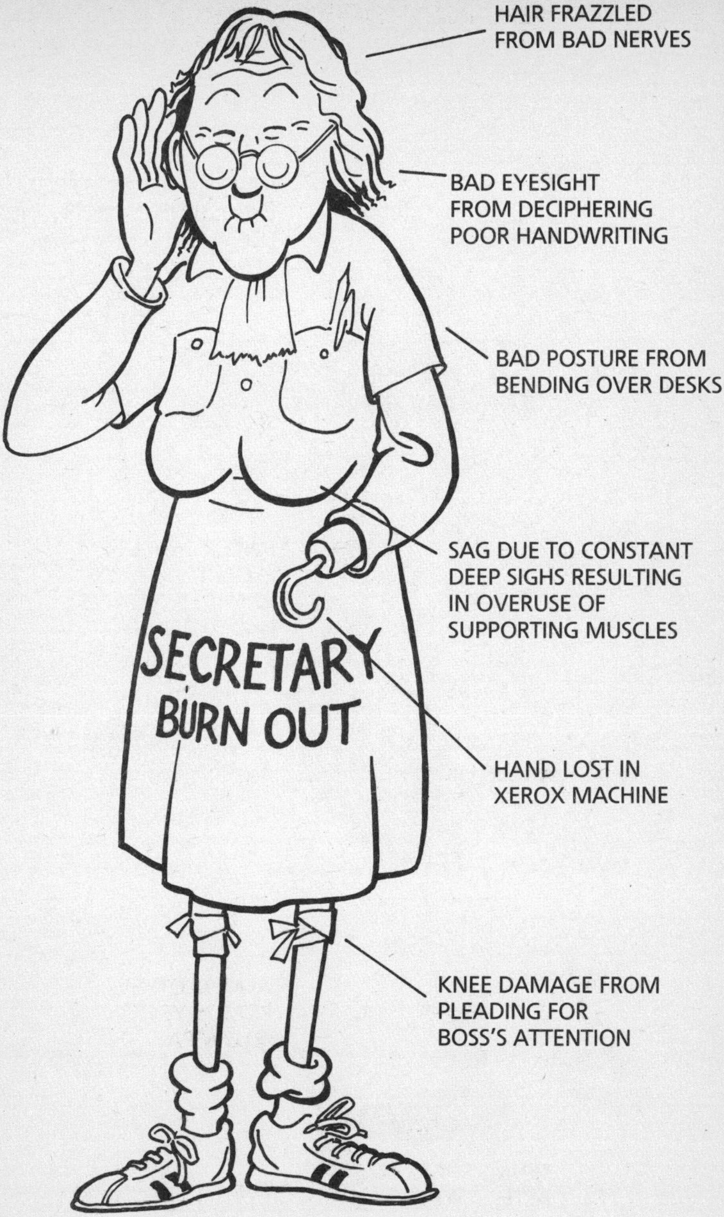
HAIR FRAZZLED FROM BAD NERVES
BAD EYESIGHT FROM DECIPHERING POOR HANDWRITING
BAD POSTURE FROM BENDING OVER DESKS
SAG DUE TO CONSTANT DEEP SIGHS RESULTING IN OVERUSE OF SUPPORTING MUSCLES
SECRETARY BURN OUT
HAND LOST IN XEROX MACHINE
KNEE DAMAGE FROM PLEADING FOR BOSS'S ATTENTION

NO UNAUTHORISED DISCLOSURES

Protect Classified Information

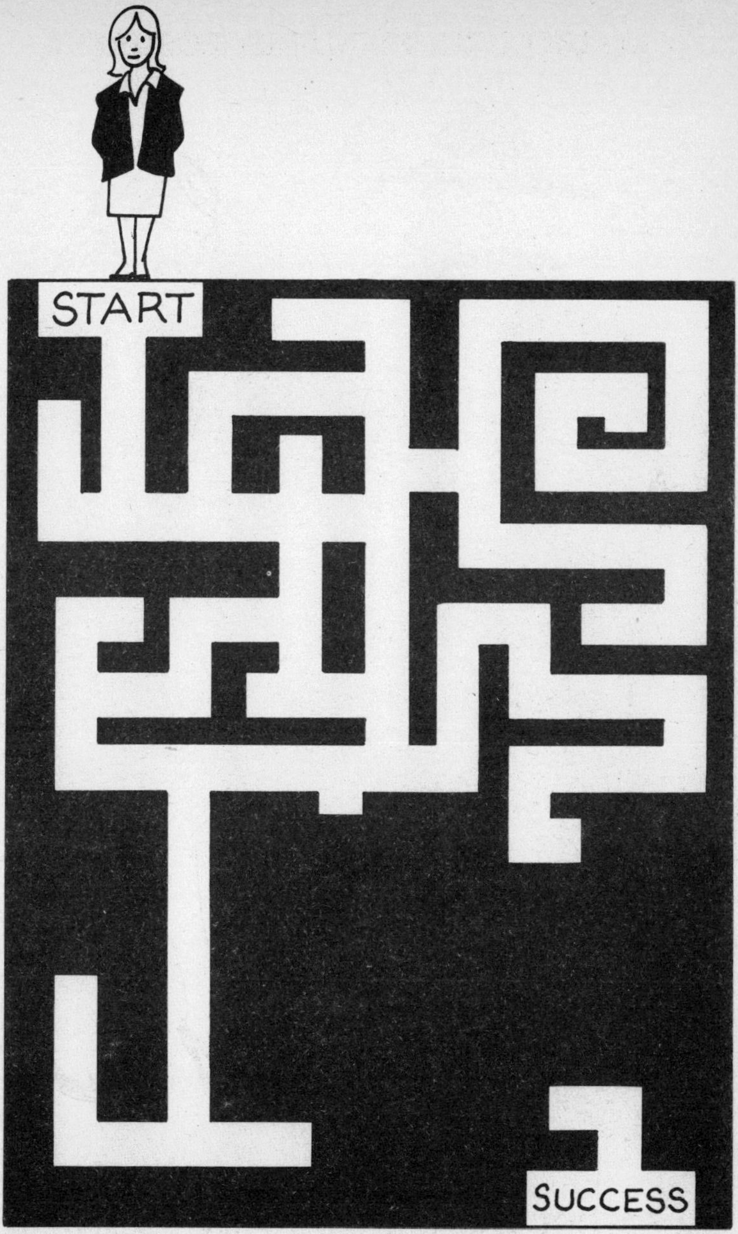
START
SUCCESS

CHAPTER 4

For the Working Woman

OCCUPATIONAL RESEARCH
IS LIKE SEX.
WHEN IT'S GOOD
IT'S GOOD —
AND WHEN IT'S
BAD, IT'S BETTER
THAN NOTHING.

In this area
sexual harrassment
will NOT be reported,
but . . .
it WILL be graded.

A Woman Has
To Do Twice As Much
As A Man To Be
Considered Half
As Good.

Fortunately,
It Isn't Difficult.

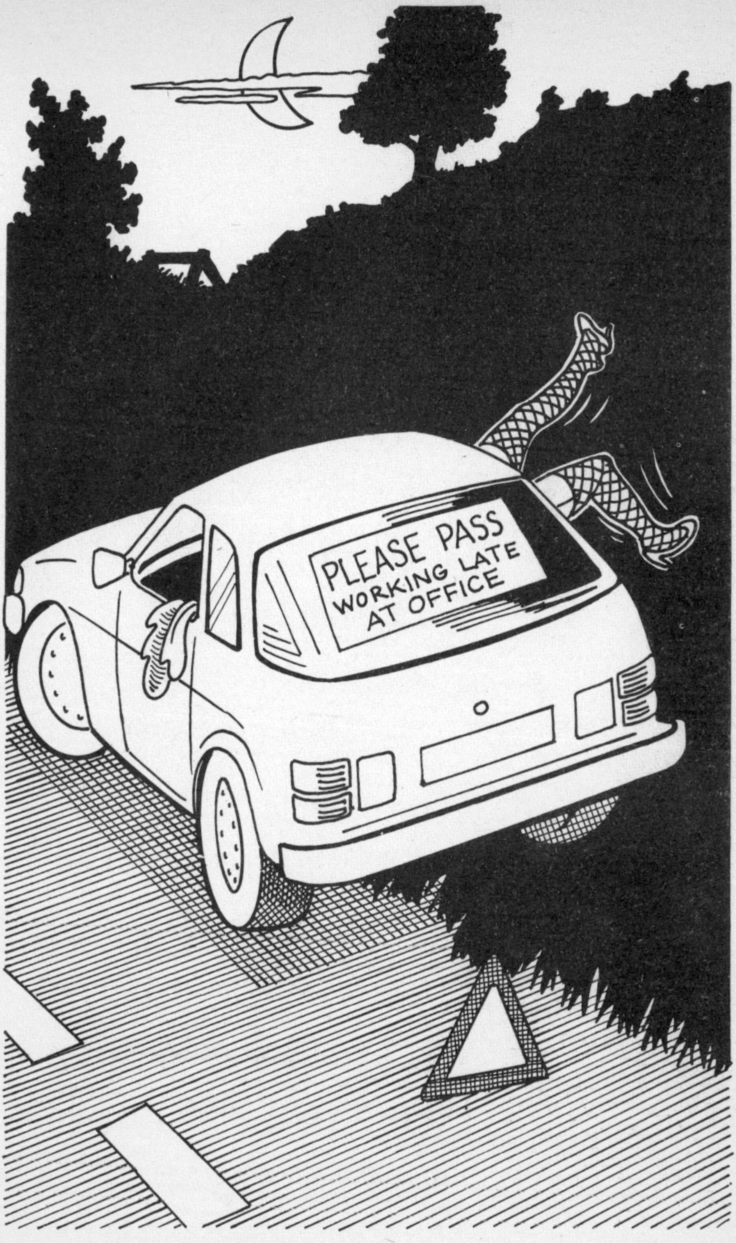
PLEASE PASS
WORKING LATE
AT OFFICE

H.G.V. Lorry Drivers' HIGHWAY CODE

When should you use your headlights?
To warn your mates of a speedtrap.

When do you overtake on the left?
When the bastard in front won't move over.

What documents do you take on the road?
Daily Mirror; Sun; Playboy and Forum.

When must you stop?
To have a piss, leg over or a tot of brandy.

Where should you not park?
Outside the house of the tart you are screwing.

What would you expect to find on a rural road?
Rural tarmac.

How many types of pedestrian crossings are there?
Those who do and those that don't.

What is the correct procedure for overtaking on a motorway?
Foot hard down, eyes shut and smile.

When should you use the fast lane on a motorway?
When you're going home on a promise.

What do you do in the event of a breakdown on the motorway?
Leave the fucking thing and hitch a lift home.

What does a yellow box junction mean?
They have run out of white paint.

What do broken white lines mean in the road?
Careless navvies.

When can you cross double white lines in the road?
After 9 lagers; 2 vodkas and a whisky

How do you avoid drowsiness on a motorway?
Finger your hitch-hiker.

What must you check before leaving a building site?
That you have enough timber under the sheet for a new kitchen cabinet.

What do double yellow lines on the side of a road mean?
Chinese takeaway ahead.

Where do you situate your danger triangle when you break down?
Up the transport manager's arse.

**YOU HAVE JUST PASSED
YOUR H.G.V. TEST**

*She used up all her sick time
so she had to call in dead this morning*

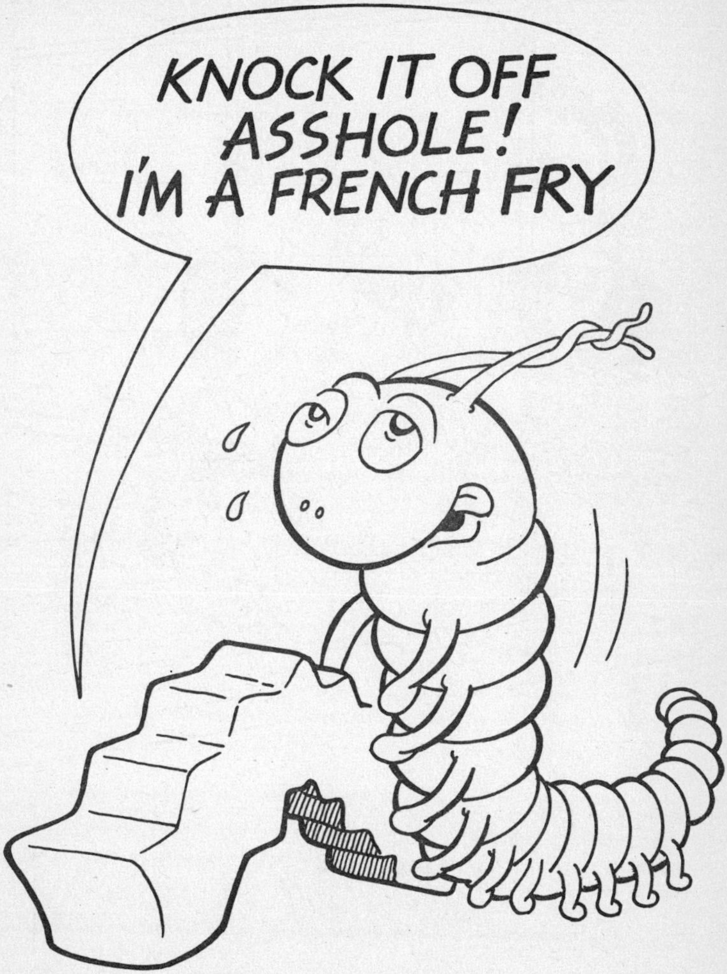
KNOCK IT OFF
ASSHOLE!
I'M A FRENCH FRY

INSPIRATIONAL WORDS FROM

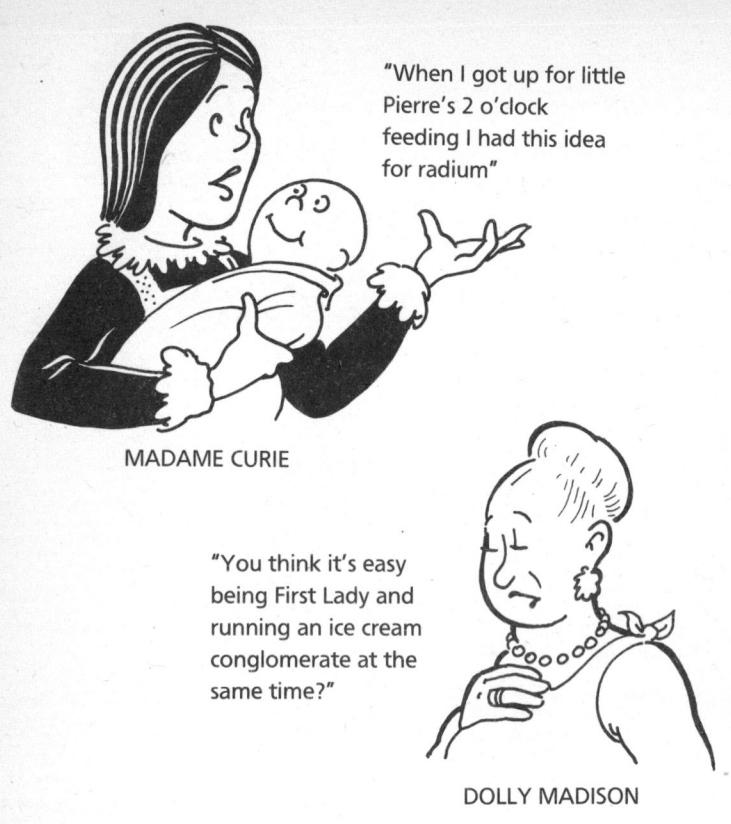

"When I got up for little Pierre's 2 o'clock feeding I had this idea for radium"

MADAME CURIE

"You think it's easy being First Lady and running an ice cream conglomerate at the same time?"

DOLLY MADISON

"I'm sorry the house is a mess. But I've got to finish this flag before they start the revolution."

BETSY ROSS

FAMOUS WORKING WOMEN

"I was one of the first women in banking"

MA BARKER

"Keeping singing. We'll be bigger than the Jackson Five."

MARIA VON TRAPP

"I'm ruling Portugal and who do you think is watching Chris's kids while he's away?"

QUEEN ISABELLA

FAMOUS QUOTATIONS FROM MALE

"Your department is running beautifully. Too bad you're not my secretary."

"You didn't reach your sales quota last week. Was it that time of the month?"

"I like you. You don't act like a woman at all."

WORKING WOMAN'S BOSSES

"Someday this company will have a female on the Board of Directors . . . and she'll have *you* to thank for paving the way."

"I personally am not a male chauvinist but a lot of the men here are."

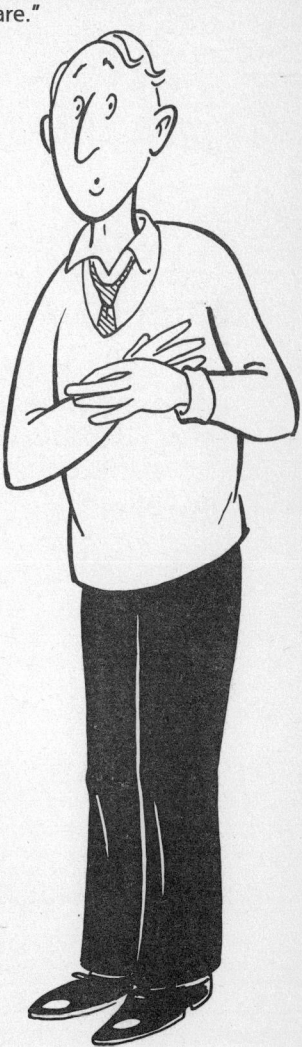

STRESS DIET

BREAKFAST
½ grapefruit
1 slice whole wheat toast
8 oz skim milk

LUNCH
4 oz. lean broiled chicken breast
1 cup steamed zucchini
1 oreo cookie
herb tea

MID-AFTERNOON SNACK
Rest of the package of Oreos
1 quart Rocky Road ice cream
1 jar hot fudge

DINNER
2 loaves garlic bread
Large pepperoni and mushroom pizza
Large pitcher of beer
2 Milky Way's
Entire frozen cheesecake eaten directly from the freezer

DIET TIPS

1. If no one sees you eat it, it has no calories.

2. If you drink a diet soda with a candy bar they cancel each other out.

3. Food used for medicinal purposes NEVER counts, such as: Hot Chocolate, Brandy, Toast, and Sara Lee Cheesecake.

4. If you fatten up everyone else around you — then you look thinner.

5. Movie related foods don't count because they are simply part of the entire entertainment experience and not a part of one's personal fuel, such as Milk Duds, Popcorn with butter, Junior Mints, and Red Licorice.

The only difference between a man and a woman climbing the ladder of success...

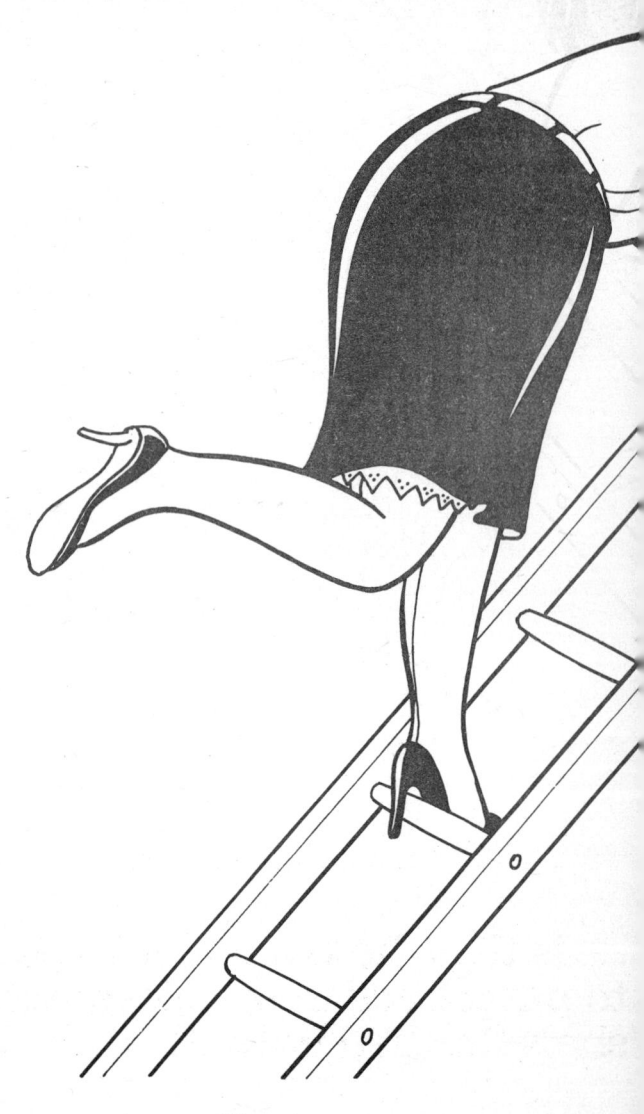

... is that the woman is expected to put it back in the closet when she's finished with it.

HOW YOU KNOW YOU'RE GROWING OLDER...

Everything hurts and what doesn't hurt doesn't work.

The gleam in your eyes is from the sun hitting your bifocals.

You feel like the night before and you haven't been anywhere.

Your little black book contains only names ending in M.D.

You get winded playing chess.

Your children begin to look middle aged.

You join a health club and don't go.

You begin to outlive enthusiasm.

Your mind makes contracts your body can't meet.

You know all the answers, but nobody asks you the questions.

You look forward to a dull evening.

Your favourite part of the newspaper is "25 years ago today".

Expose yourself to computing

THE AGES OF WOMEN

There are five geographic ages of women:

1. Between the ages of 16 and 18, she is like Africa, virgin and unexplored.

2. Between the ages of 19 and 35, she is like Asia, hot and exotic.

3. Between the ages of 36 and 45, she is like America, fully explored and free with her resources.

4. Between the ages of 46 and 56, she is like Europe, exhausted but still has points of interest.

5. After 56, she is like Australia, everybody knows it's down there but nobody gives a damn.

CHAPTER 5

For the Working Man

WHAT'S ON A MAN'S MIND

*Here is a fellow who really takes care of his body —
He lifts weights and jogs 5 miles a day —
One morning he looked in the mirror and admired his body —
He noticed he is tanned all over — except his penis and decided to do something about that —
He went to the beach, undressed and buried himself in the sand, except for his penis.
Two little old ladies were strolling along the beach. One looked down and said, "There is really no justice in this world."
The other lady said, "You're right, look at that."
When I was 10 years old, I was afraid of it.
When I was 20 years old, I was curious about it.
When I was 30 years old, I enjoyed it.
When I was 40 years old, I asked for it.
When I was 50 years old, I paid for it.
When I was 60 years old, I prayed for it.
When I was 70 years old, I forgot about it.
And now that I'm 80 years old, the darn things are growing wild.*

Yeah, Yeah, course I love ya'

THE WORKING GIRL'S DOODLE PAD

Here's to moments of sweet repose,
   It's tummy to tummy and toes to toes
But after that moment of sweet delight
   It's fanny to fanny the rest of the night.

FLY

UNITED

THE STORY OF TWENTY TOES

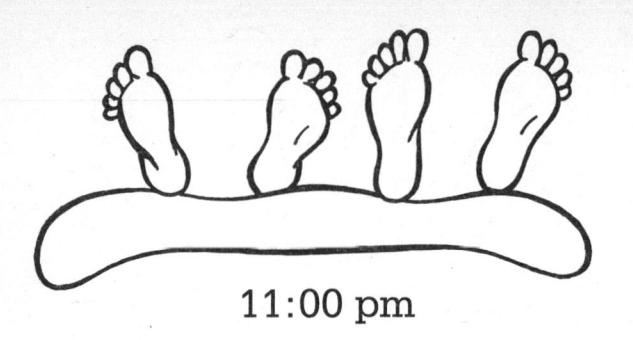

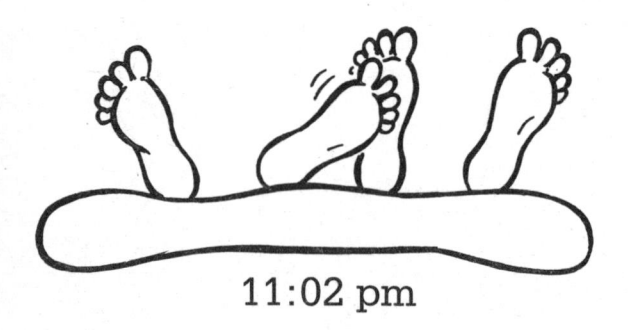

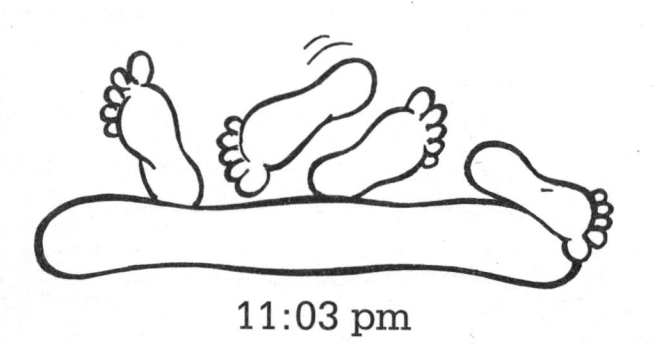

11:00 pm

11:02 pm

11:03 pm

TOLD IN TWENTY MINUTES

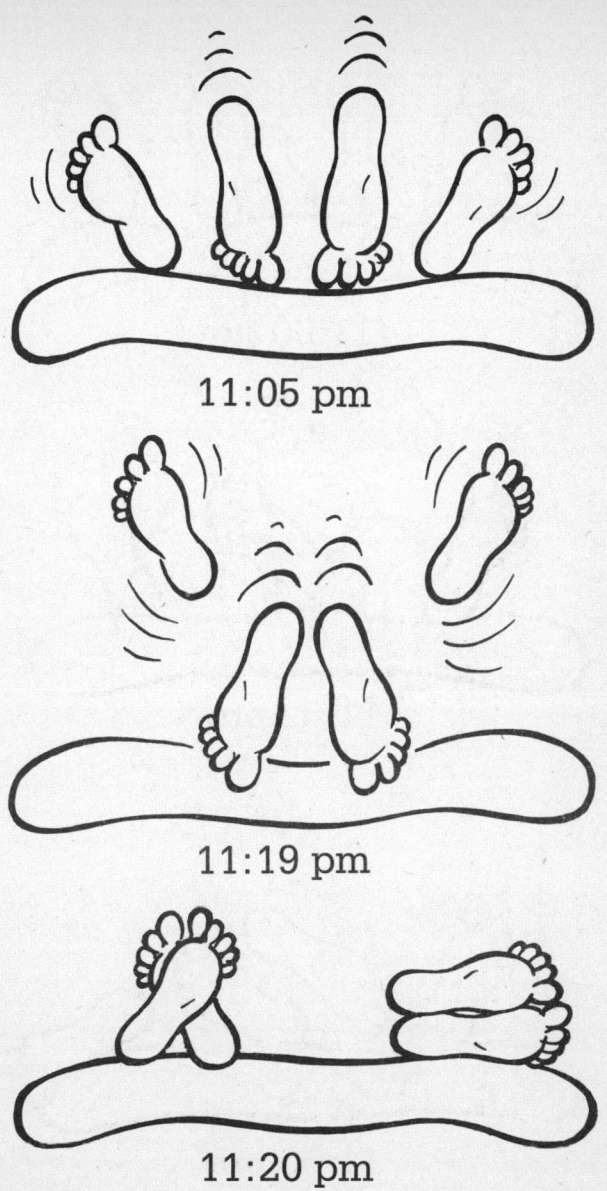

11:05 pm

11:19 pm

11:20 pm

*Once a King
Always a King
But Once
a Knight
is Enough*

CHAPTER 6

International Relations

POLISH SEX

HANDBOOK

→ IN →

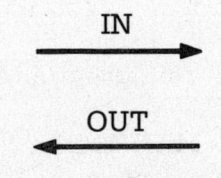

← OUT ←

REPEAT IF NECESSARY

OFFICIAL POLISH SEX QUIZ

TRUE/FALSE

1. A clitoris is a type of flower _____
2. A pubic hair is a wild rabbit _____
3. A vulva is an automobile from Sweden _____
4. The term "spread eagle" is an extinct bird _____
5. A fallopian tube is part of a television _____
6. It is dangerous to have a wet dream under an electric blanket _____
7. Copulation is sex between two consenting policemen _____
8. McDonald's golden arches is a phallus symbol _____
9. A vagina is a medical term used to describe heart trouble _____
10. A menstrual cycle has three wheels _____
11. Fellatio is an Italian dagger _____
12. A G-string is a weapon used by G-men _____
13. Semen is a term for sailors _____
14. An anus is a Greek word denoting a period of time _____
15. Testicles are found on an octopus _____
16. Cunnilingus is a person who can speak four languages _____
17. Asphalt is a medical term used to describe someone with rectal problems _____
18. KOTEX is a radio station in Dallas, Texas _____
19. Masturbate is something used to catch large fish _____
20. Coitus is a musical instrument _____
21. Foetus is a character in Gunsmoke _____
22. An umbilical cord is part of a parachute _____
23. A condom is an apartment complex _____
24. A rectum is what you are for taking this test _____

"BLOODY YANKS"

Is tomorrow good enough for you?

FRANCE

Arab terrorist   Irish terrorist

American terrorist

CHAPTER 7

You're Never Too Old (And You're Never Too Young)

SO WHAT'S SO GREAT ABOUT SLEEPING TOGETHER ?

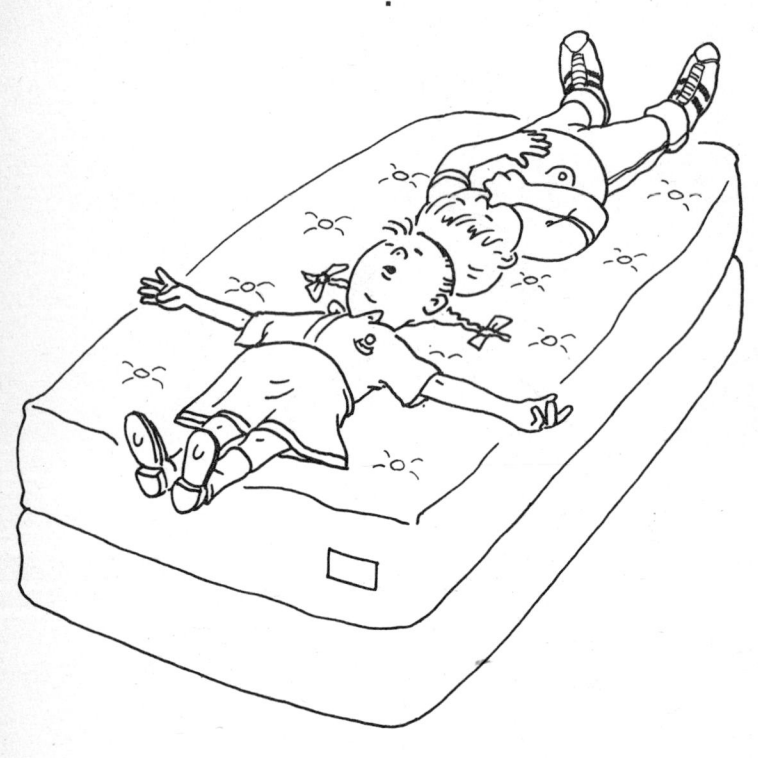

"Okay, we took off our clothes...
I got on top of you... how soon
till it starts to feel good?"

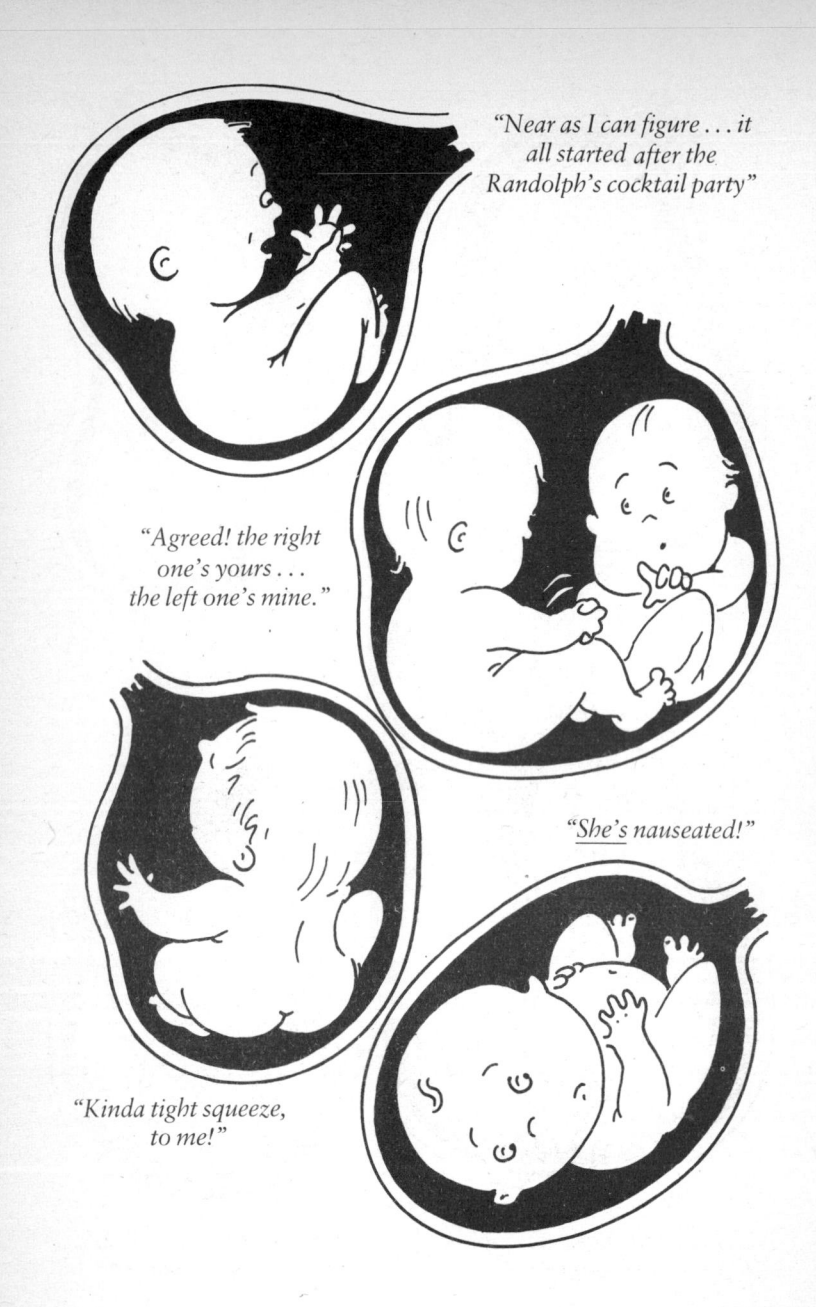

"Near as I can figure ... it all started after the Randolph's cocktail party"

"Agreed! the right one's yours ... the left one's mine."

"She's nauseated!"

"Kinda tight squeeze, to me!"

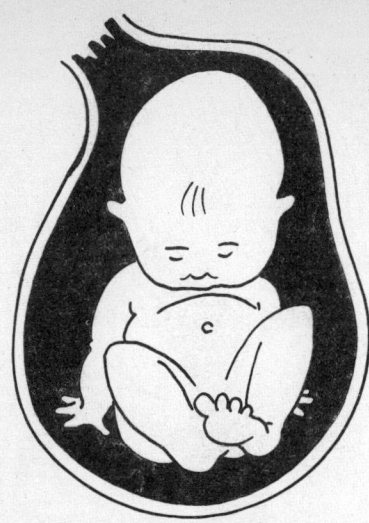

"Who's calling who Mary Lou!"

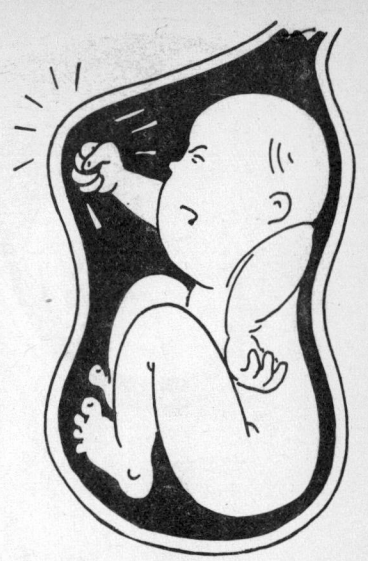

"How many times do I gotta tell her not to cross her legs!"

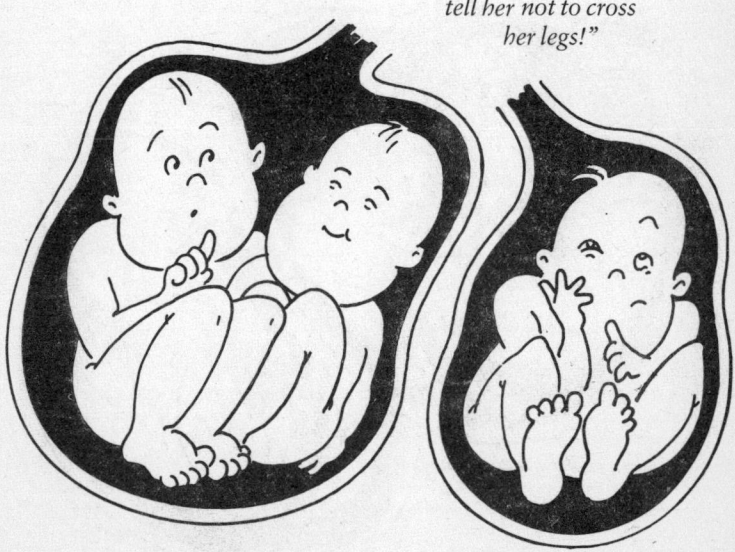

"Now, remember! Last one out yells 'surprise'!"

"One more kiss like that and I'll be having company!"

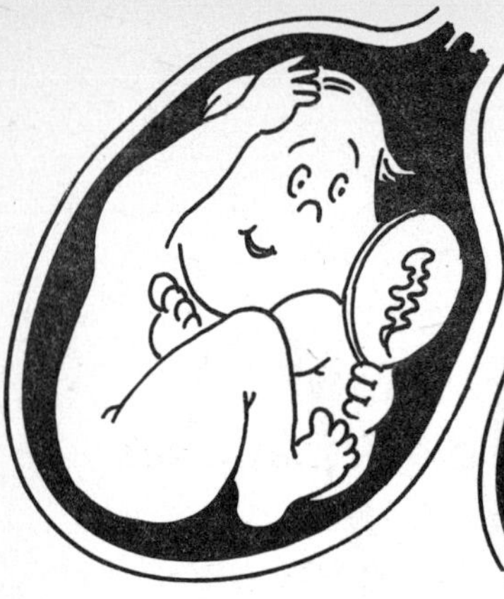

"Better spruce up . . . today's my coming-out party"

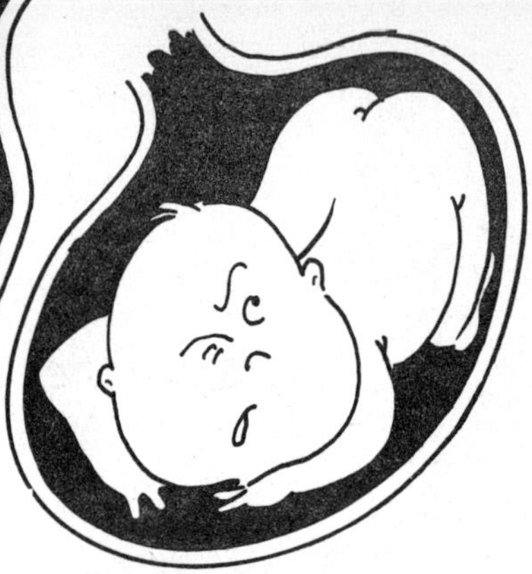

"What the hell's he mean . . . A well-formed head?"

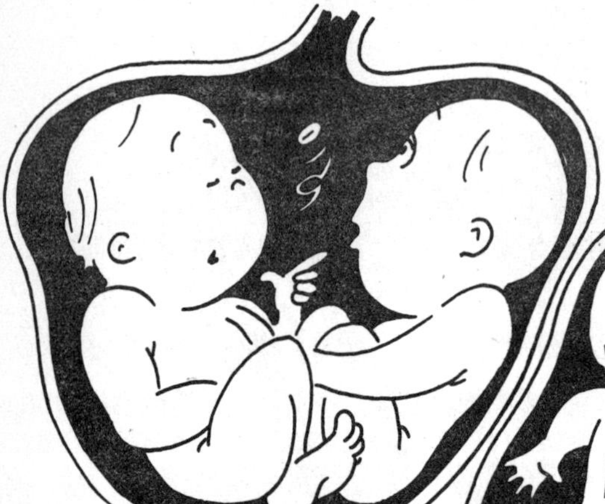

"Heads, I go first!"

"I'm coming! I'm coming! Put down that scalpel"

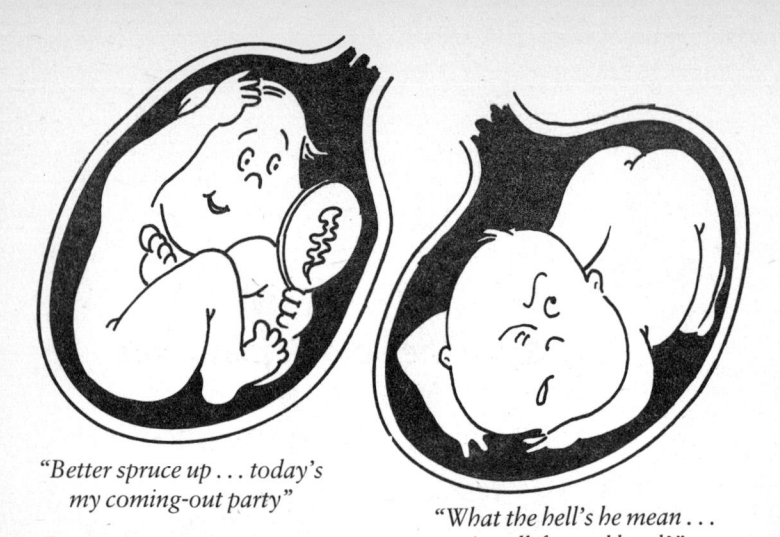

*How come they didn't play cards
on Noah's Ark?*
Because Noah sat on the deck.

*Did you know that Noah took dollars on
board the Ark?*
The duck took a bill.
The frog took a greenback.
And the skunk took a cent.

*What did Noah say when his sons wanted
to fish?*
"Don't go overboard with the worms.
We only have two."

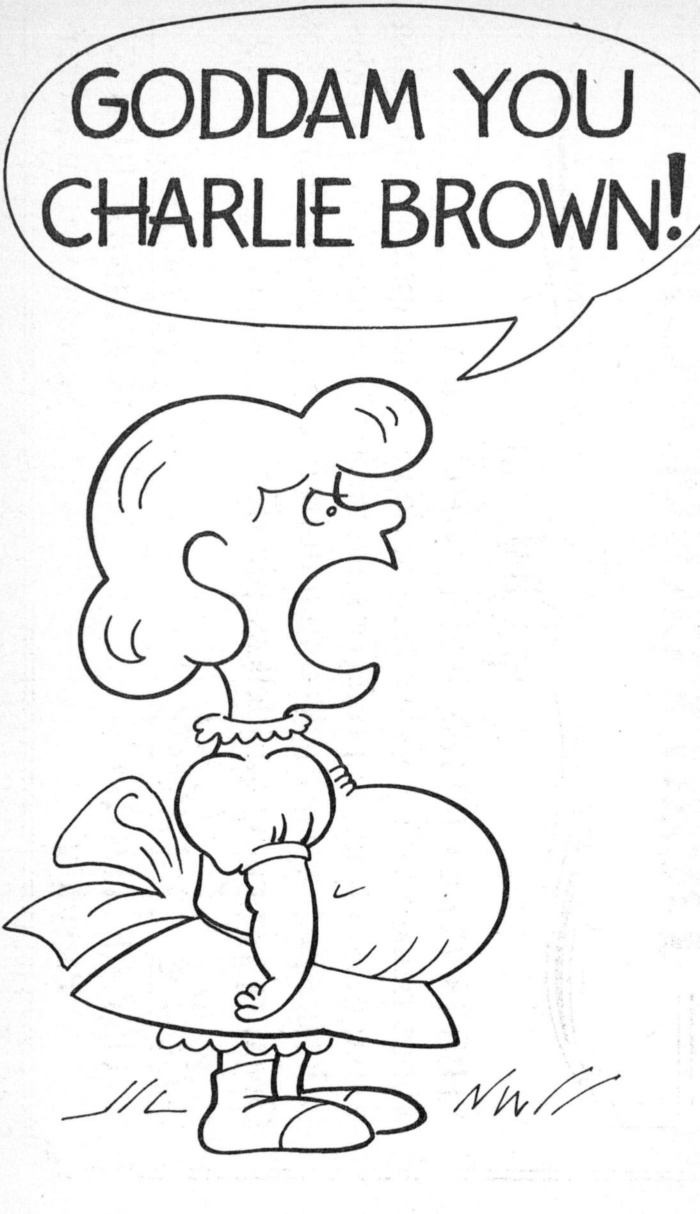
GODDAM YOU CHARLIE BROWN!

Dead Pekkers Club

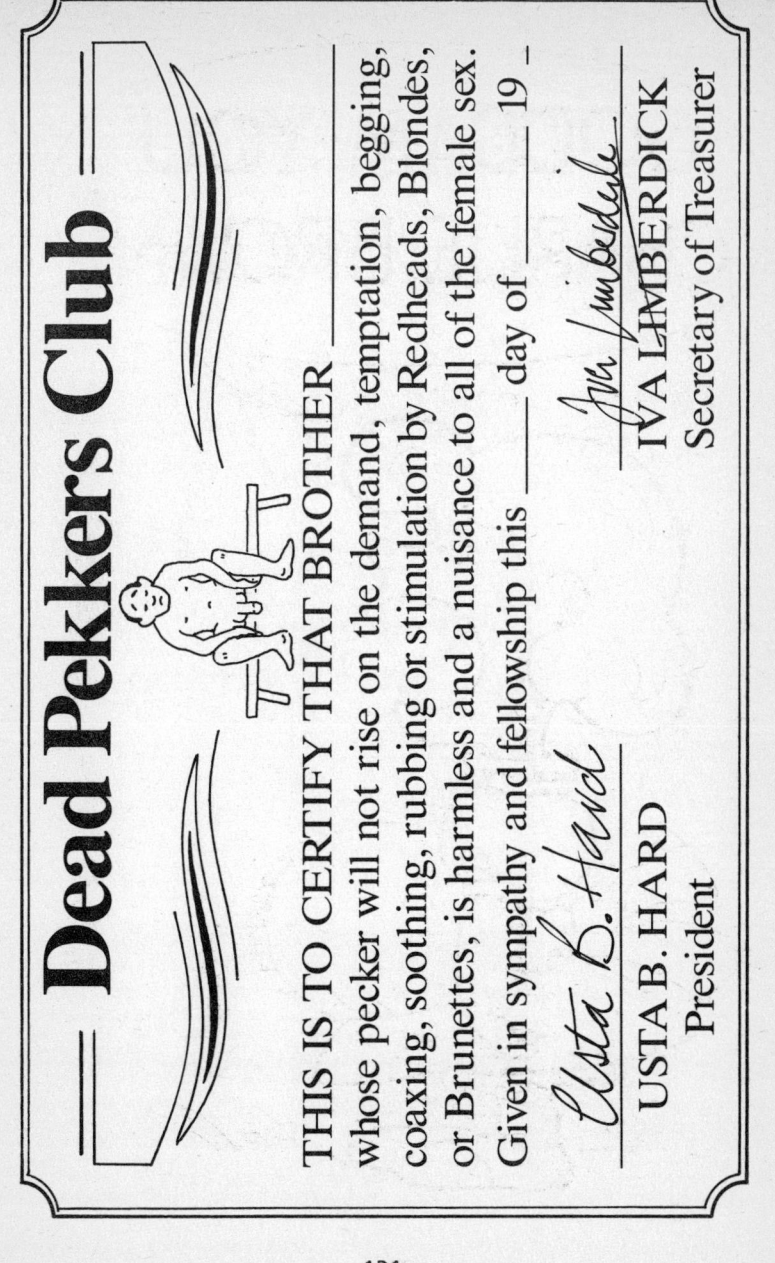

THIS IS TO CERTIFY THAT BROTHER _____ whose pecker will not rise on the demand, temptation, begging, coaxing, soothing, rubbing or stimulation by Redheads, Blondes, or Brunettes, is harmless and a nuisance to all of the female sex. Given in sympathy and fellowship this ____ day of ____ 19 __

Usta B. Hard
USTA B. HARD
President

Iva Limberdick
IVA LIMBERDICK
Secretary of Treasurer

This is to certify that

____

has the indicated number of days to go before retirement

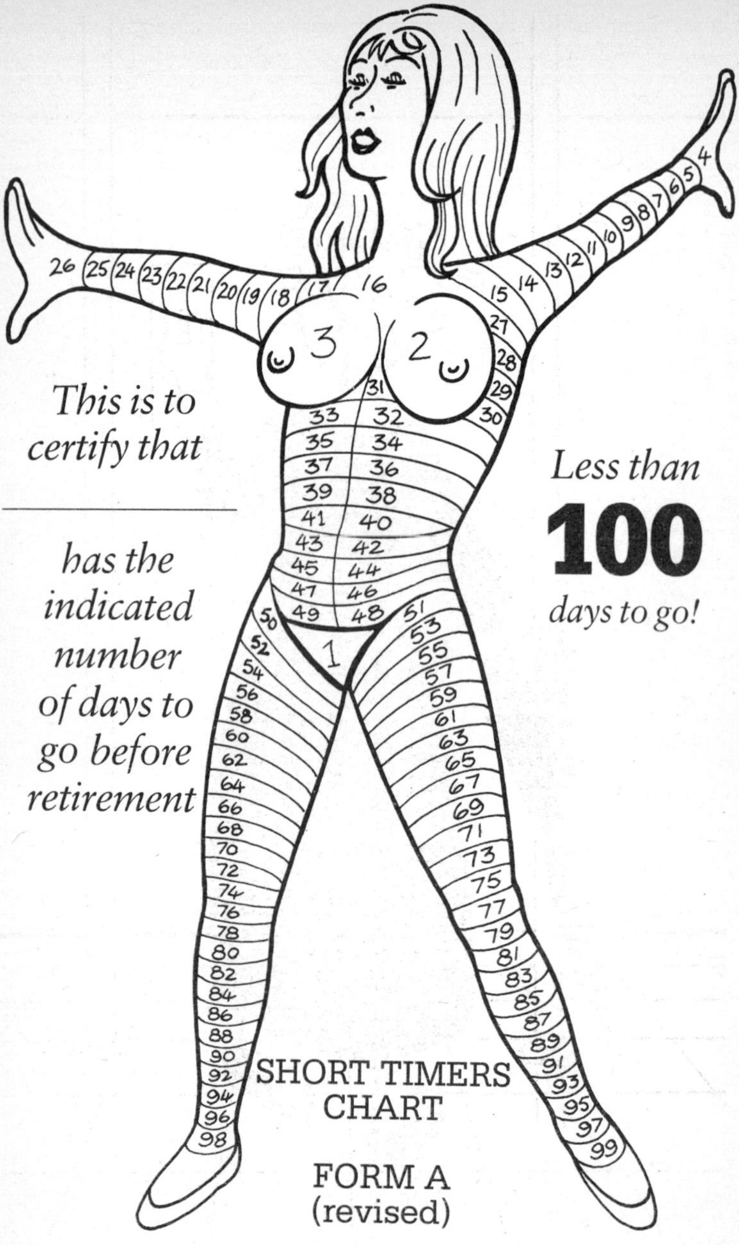

Less than

100

days to go!

SHORT TIMERS CHART

FORM A
(revised)

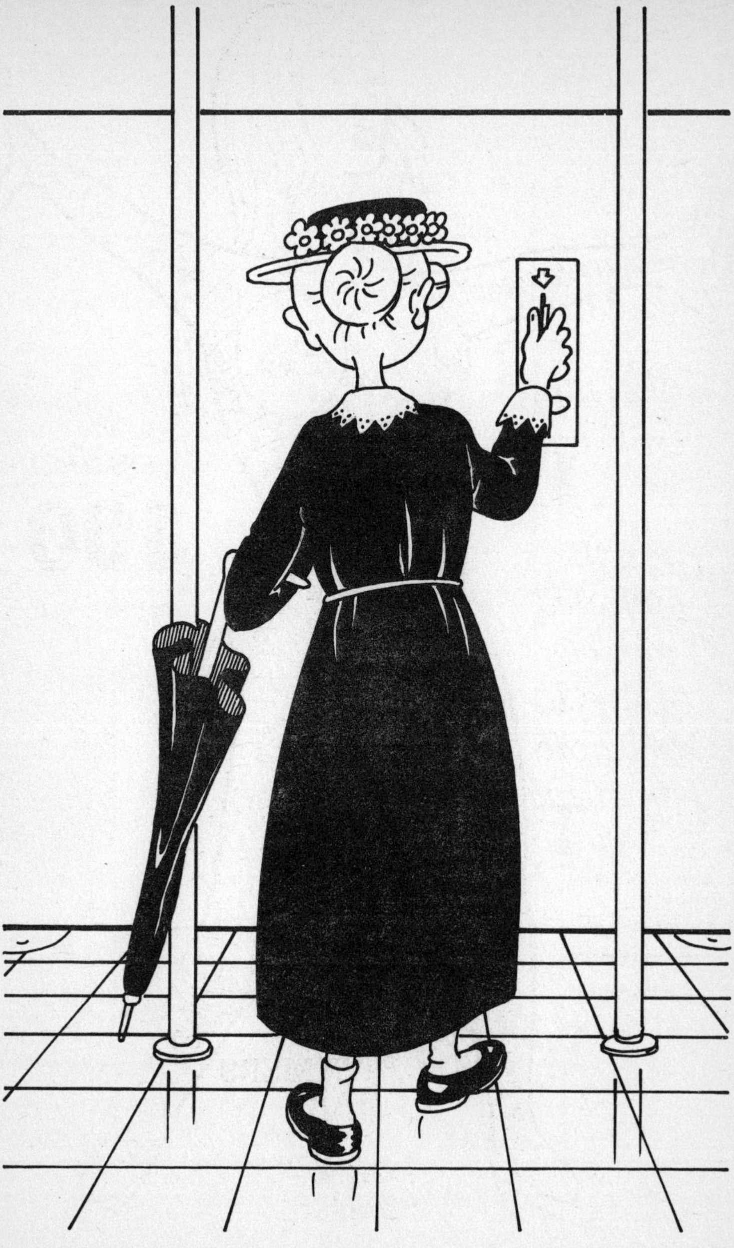

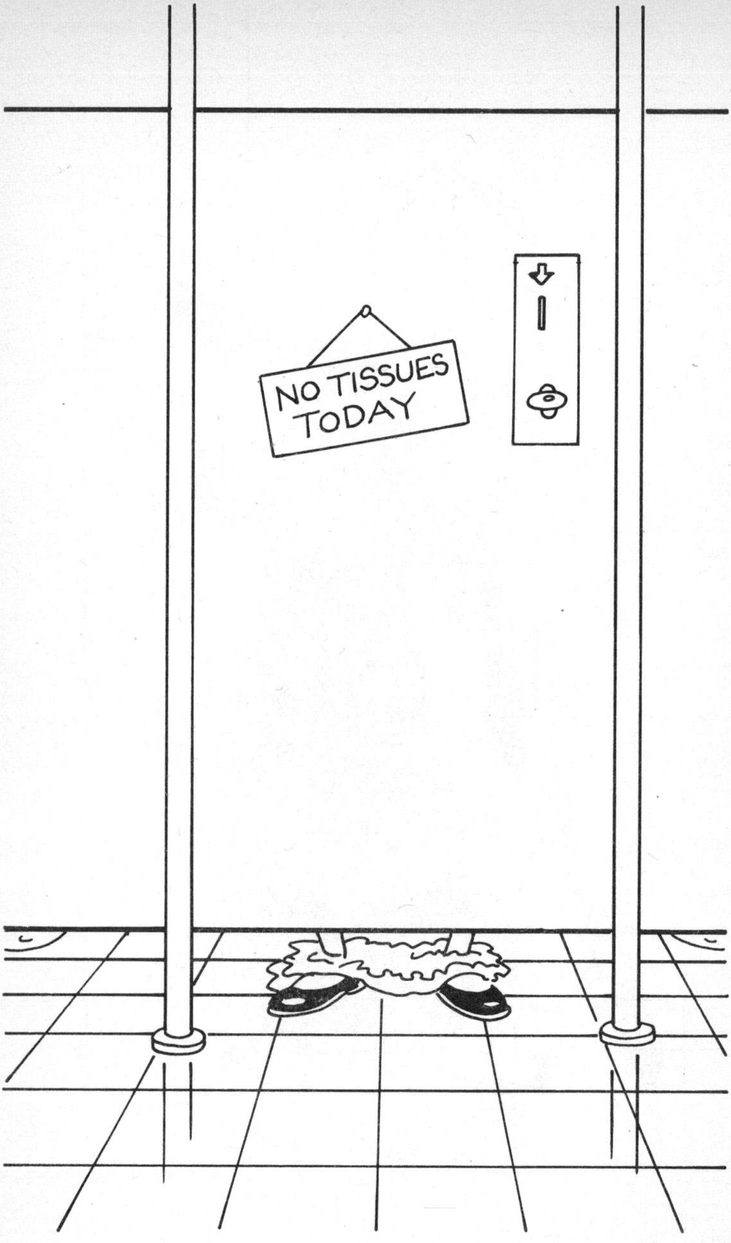
NO TISSUES
TODAY

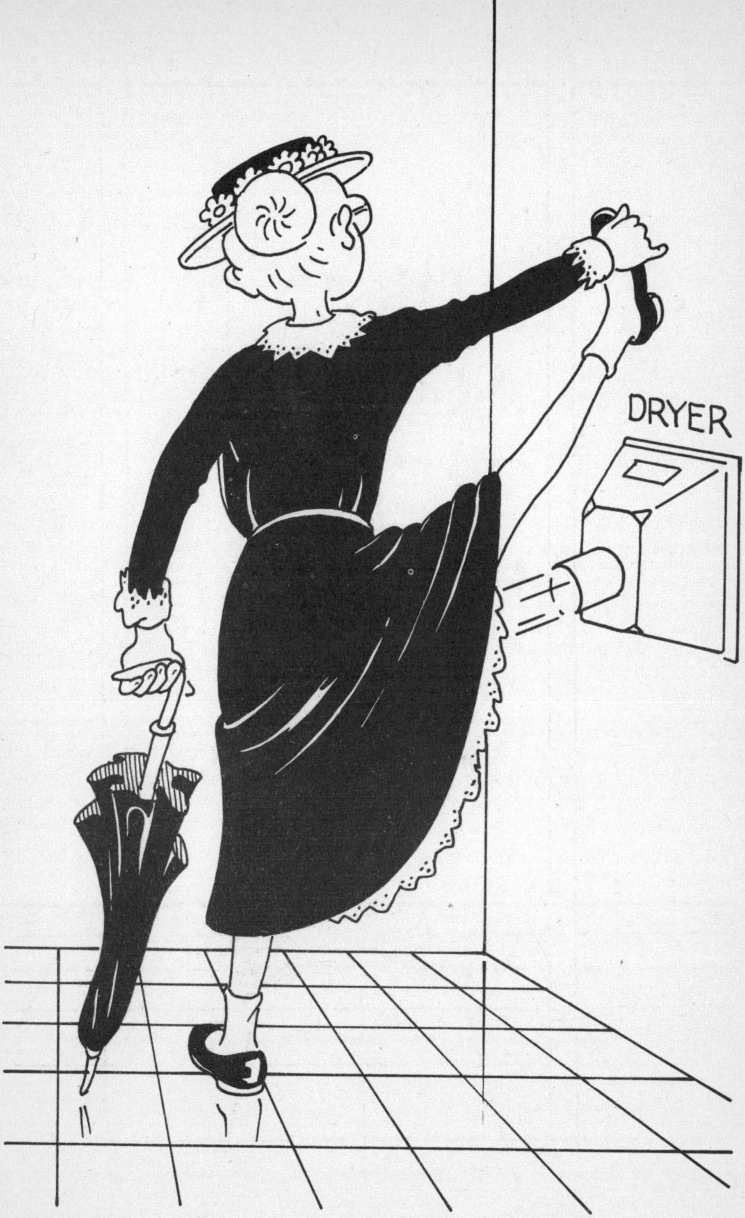
DRYER

OKAY
SO GOD
CREATED
THE EARTH
IN
SEVEN DAYS

(but he didn't have to do it in triplicate)

CHAPTER 8

Belts from the Bible

NOAH'S WAY

And the Lord said unto Noah, "Where is the ark I commanded thee to build?"

And Noah said unto the Lord, "Verily, I have had three carpenters off ill. The gopher-wood supplier hath let me down — yea, even though the gopher-wood hath been on order for nigh upon 12 months. What can I do, O Lord?"

And God said unto Noah, "I want that ark finished after seven days and seven nights."

And Noah said, "It will be so." And it was not so.

And the Lord said unto Noah, "What seemeth to be the trouble this time?"

And Noah said unto the Lord, "Mine subcontractor hath gone bankrupt. The pitch which thou commanded me to put on the inside and on the outside of the ark hath not arrived. The plumber hath gone on strike. Shem, my son who helpeth me on the ark side of business, hath formed a pop group with his brothers Ham and Japhet. Lord, I am undone."

And the Lord grew angry and said, "And what about the animals, the male and the female of every sort that I ordered to come unto thee to keep their seed alive upon the face of the earth?"

And Noah said, "They have been delivered unto the wrong address but should be arriving on Friday."

And the Lord said, "How about the unicorns, and the fowls of the air by sevens?"

And Noah wrung his hands and wept, saying, "Lord, unicorns are a discontinued line.

Thou canst not get them for love nor money. And fowls of the air are sold only in half-dozens. Lord, Lord, thou knowest how it is."

And the Lord in his wisdom said, "Noah, my son, I knowest. Why else dost thou think I have caused a flood to descend upon the earth?"

December 11, 1988

Dear Mr. Claus

I received your letter of December 1, 1988, and can really sympathize with your predicament. "YOUR GOOD WILL and FREE GIVING SPIRIT" are admired by many far and near.

We here at the office have been watching you too, very closely! And we have compiled a list of several questions we would like you to answer.

FIRST: Where do you get all the money for the "FREE TOYS?"

SECOND: How do you pay your workers? (Elves, HUH!?!)

THIRD: Speaking of the twelve days of Christmas, are you by any chance dealing in slaves?

FOURTH: When was the last time you filed your income tax?

Sincerely

IRS Agent, Washington
D.C. District

P.S.: We have reason to believe that you transport illegal aliens across state lines, and have referred your case to the FBI, and the Department of Immigration. The Department of Motor Vehicles has been informed of your exploits, and are very interested in your vehicle registration and unlicenced animals. Oh yes, you have an appointment at our Washington Office on Tuesday at 9.00 a.m.

AND A VERY MERRY CHRISTMAS TO YOU TOO!!!

Pay attention, damn it, I said the Schmidt house!

"But Adam, who's going to take care of the plants?"

EVEN TODAY!

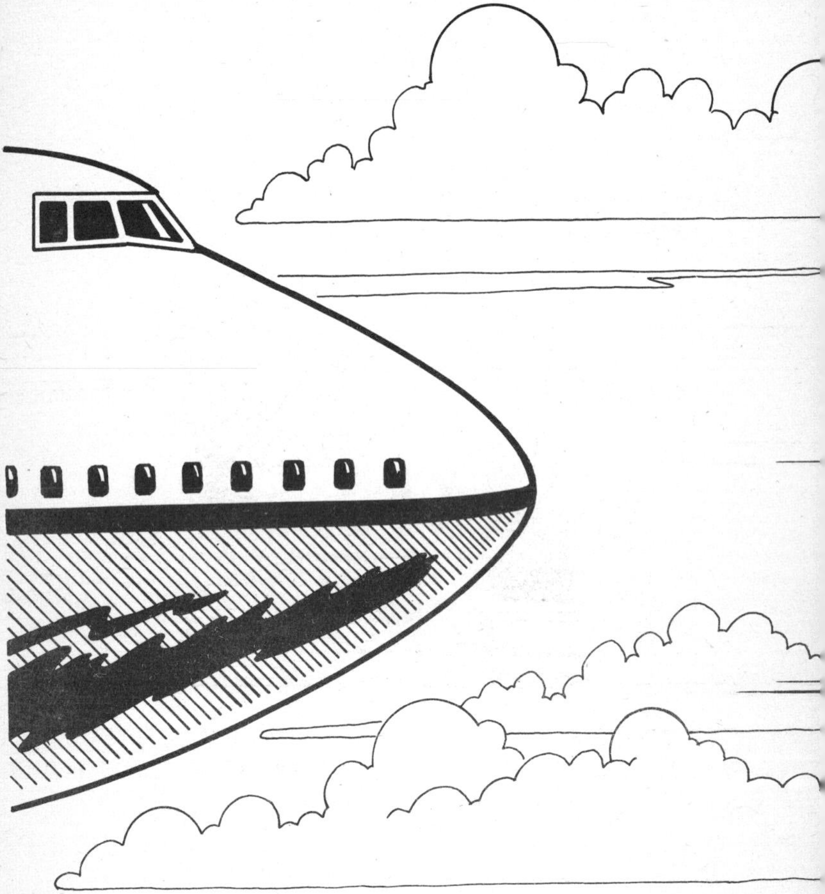

DAMN 747s!

The wise men see the star

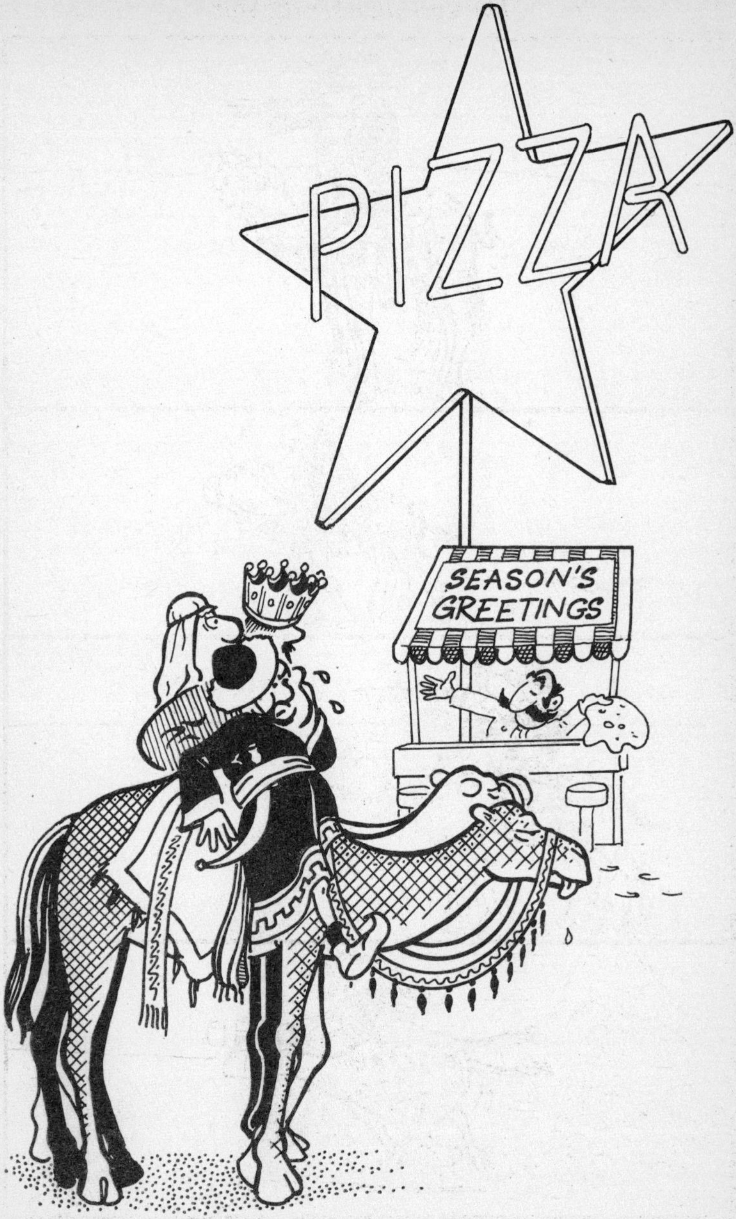
PIZZA
SEASON'S GREETINGS

TENNIS Quiz Book

Ian Thomson & Mansel Davies

Anyone for tennis?...

At last, the definitive quiz book for the tennis enthusiast who prefers an armchair challenge to an 'on-court' one!

With 1,000 questions ranging from the less taxing:

Who did John McEnroe beat in 1981 to win his first Men's Singles title at the Wimbledon Championships?

Which tournament is traditionally played a fortnight before Wimbledon at London's Queen's Club?

– to those for the hardiest challenger:

Who was the Wimbledon champion who won an Olympic Silver medal in Ice Hockey?

Who, during 1976, became the first European player to pass $1 million in career earnings?

You'll find the TENNIS QUIZ BOOK a formidable opponent with many devious shots to fool and confuse you. But don't be discouraged – in this game, it's guile that gains, not ground play!

And don't miss the other *Quiz Books* in the series:
GOLF QUIZ BOOK
CRICKET QUIZ BOOK
FOOTBALL QUIZ BOOK

0 7474 0110 1   QUIZ   £2.50

THE PALACE
PAUL ERDMAN

The flash of a wheel, the twinkling spin of a ball, the fat slap of a heavy wallet as glazed eyes ignite and bejewelled fingers tremble, urging that faithless harlot, Lady Luck, to stretch out and offer her all. Gambling – compelling, glamorous, sleazy and addictive – is wickedly exposed in Paul Erdman's masterly novel of financial skulduggery on the Big Game circuits. From the vast money-making centres of Las Vegas and Atlantic City to the shadowy, underground gambling dives of London and Beirut, he spins a spellbinding tale of wealth and treachery, intrigue and mob conspiracy. Proud, aristocratic international bankers, sharp-eyed card tricksters, corrupt politicians, professional criminals are all in on the game in this devastatingly suspenseful, cracking-paced thriller that will have you hooked from first page to last . . .

'Mind-blowing financial scams . . . lively narrative spanning two decades in which fortunes are won and lost . . . very funny and very sharp'
LITERARY REVIEW

Also by Paul Erdman in Sphere Books:
THE LAST DAYS OF AMERICA
THE CRASH OF '79
THE PANIC OF '89

0 7474 0259 0   THRILLER   £3.50

BAD MONEY
A.M. KABAL

'Midsummer's Eve, the hard men moved...'

01.01 hours GMT: in London, Rome, Panama and Gdansk four men are savagely murdered. No one sees the connection. It's a quiet, efficient start to the international crime of the century...

But one victim, reporter Tom Wellbeck, leaves behind his ex-wife, fellow-journalist Caro Kilkenny, who is determined to find the truth about his death. And then there's Tom's friend, John Standing – burned-out, alcoholic, but still the one man with the skill and experience to see the case through...

They unravel a thread of intrigue that stretches from Warsaw to Washington, from the silent corridors of the Vatican to the murderous jungles of Central America, a vicious thread of bad blood and bad money. And when Standing detects the hand of his old enemy David Medina, he knows their troubles are just beginning...

Financial devilry of a high order... knowledgeable and sinister
OBSERVER

Also by A M Kabal in Sphere Books:
THE ADVERSARY

0 7221 5232 9   CRIME/THRILLER   £3.99

JUNIPER
James Murphy

'Knowing your enemy is not the primary consideration. You have to know what you are defending first of all. Then the enemy will show itself.'

Oliver Maitland joined MI5 to defend his country. To defend freedom and democracy. He's served his time in the hell of Northern Ireland, battling for a peaceful solution. Now he's transferred to counter-subversion, fighting, not the IRA but ordinary men and women.

Phone tapping, mail interception, burglary – it's a dirty war. And when Maitland finds out the truth behind the Mountbatten murder he begins to wonder who the enemy really is.

Operation JUNIPER, brainchild of Maitland's sadistic boss, 'The Butcher', is the deadliest campaign yet. It's going to smash the peace movement and sabotage disarmament talks. Maitland knows the butcher doesn't care how many British agents have to die to fulfil his plans. What he doesn't know is that he's top of the hit-list . . .

Also by James Murphy in Sphere Books:

CEDAR

WILDTRACK

BERNARD CORNWELL

After the hell of the Falklands War, Nick Sandman, VC, knows what it is to be a hero. Barely able to walk, he's got no money, no job and no prospects. But, defiantly, he clings to the memory of a boat called *Sycorax*, his only possession, his only hope of a life at sea with no rules and no fighting. Until even that dream is shattered . . .

For there is no *Sycorax* to return to – only a beached and battered wreck, torn from its Devon mooring. In its place stands the gleaming ocean racer *Wildtrack*. And into Nick's life comes its menacing owner Tony Bannister, a rich and powerful TV personality. Compelled to make a desperate bargain with the ruthless Bannister, Nick is forced into a deal which may give him a chance to reclaim his dream – but at a price. And in the murky world of deceit and fraud into which Nick is thrown, that price could be his own life . . .

Also by Bernard Cornwell in Sphere Books:
REDCOAT

0 7474 0187 X   GENERAL FICTION   £3.50

St Peter's Finger

GLADYS MITCHELL

A child is found dead in a bath at a nearby convent. Death, said the coroner, was caused by poisoning. The inquest returned a verdict of suicide. But Mrs Bradley is having none of that. She soon detects that she has a murder on her hands – the murder of an heiress to a fortune. Her thorough (and thoroughly original) investigation reveals that several people stand to benefit from the girl's death. Even the distressed nuns . . .

The inimitable Mrs (later Dame) Beatrice Adela Lestrange Bradley – of the clawlike grip and horrid leer – Home Office psychiatric consultant and eccentric sleuth, tackles her most macabre mystery yet.

Also by Gladys Mitchell in Sphere Books:
SUNSET OVER SOHO
THE DEVIL'S ELBOW
LAMENT FOR LETO